A much-needed follow-up to his *Character and*
Oxenham's new book, *Character and Virtue in*
helps leaders work through issues related to
With its emphasis on community engagement and contextual relevance, it is
an essential resource for training pastors and emerging leaders in Majority
World contexts to serve with wisdom, compassion and integrity.

Nigel Ajay Kumar, PhD
Theological Education Consultant and Curriculum Designer,
Global Theological Education Network

This is an excellent workbook that I highly recommend. This workbook answers
an urgent need within the Christian community for practical materials to
advance character and virtues. There is no better place to start for a balanced,
thorough and thoughtful introduction to the practice of Christian character
and virtues.

James Arthur, DPhil
Director Emeritus,
Jubilee Centre for Character and Virtues, University of Birmingham, UK

I have tacitly assumed that the character of leaders emerges organically
from a combination of discipleship, theological studies, spiritual formation,
mentoring and modelling. While all of these elements have their place,
it is widely acknowledged that something is amiss. Simply lamenting the
deficiencies in the character of leaders in our societies and churches without
critically examining our approaches to leader formation is insufficient. Marvin
Oxenham's *Character and Virtue in Practice* offers a focused and intentional
process for cultivating Christian virtue and character in leaders in a wide
variety of contexts. This workbook will assist workers around the world as
they equip leaders through individual mentoring, church-centred, non-formal
training and formal theological education.

John Bernard, DMin
President, Mesa Global

Dr. Oxenham's *Character and Virtue in Practice* is an invaluable twenty-four-
week guide designed for Christians who often try hard to be good, to mixed
results. Marvin Oxenham presents a more realistic, biblical and effective
approach: training to be good. *Character and Virtue in Practice* is a clear and

practical workbook that invites you to train like an athlete, and develop habits and virtues that will help you and those around you flourish.

René Breuel
Lead Pastor, Hopera Church, Italy
and **Sarah Breuel**
Executive Director, Revive Europe
Member of the Board of Directors, Lausanne Movement

Dr. Oxenham's *Character and Virtue in Practice* is an invaluable twenty-four-week guide designed to cultivate Christian character and virtues. With a practical approach that is adaptable to formal and non-formal settings, this book encourages the formation of lasting habits and virtues through accessible resources and biblical examples. Its flexible structure allows for learning in a variety of modalities, promoting a virtuous life that is transformative and applicable in multiple cultural contexts.

Jhohan Centeno, PhD
Theological Education Consultant,
Latin America and the Caribbean, Mesa Global

For many, virtue and character are vague categories or, at best, hard to explain. Oxenham simplifies these not only for understanding but also proposes tools to develop it. Scouring through Scripture and using examples from philosophy, culture, myth and narratives, he brings to life each virtue in a way that you would want to develop it. This is a great resource for the church.

Joyson K. Cherian, PhD
Regional Vice-President, Manna Group of Ministries
Founder Coordinator, Christ Love For All Youth Movement

Character and Virtue in Practice is a unique, interactive, multi-generational guide to virtue literacy, offering practical insights for cultivating virtuous character. It inspires personal growth and community transformation through engaging activities. I highly commend Marvin Oxenham's labour of love to you.

Samuel E. Chiang
Deputy Secretary General, World Evangelical Alliance

This insightful guide addresses a vital, but often forgotten, element of discipleship—the development of virtue. Dr. Marvin Oxenham lays out a clear path for character growth that is informed by Scripture and easily contextualized for readers around the world. Highly recommended for theological educators, pastors, church planters, new believers and all who wish to cultivate virtue in alignment with Christ.

Valerie Hamilton, PhD
Member Engagement, A Global Alliance for Church Multiplication GACX

For those committed to competency-based theological education, *Character and Virtue in Practice* offers a unique blend of biblical teaching and practical exercises designed to connect character education and discipleship. Its focus on nurturing sustained habits makes it a valuable resource for developing leaders with Christ-like integrity. As Marvin notes, the workbook is best leveraged in the context of community, which makes the communal nature of competency-based theological education a natural fit.

Greg Henson, DMin
President,
Kairos University, South Dakota, USA

Character and Virtue in Practice: A Workbook for Discipleship and Formation is an invaluable resource for anyone seeking to deepen their understanding of character and virtue. Through its structured twenty-four-week practice plan, this workbook provides practical guidance for individuals and groups alike on character formation. A perfect companion for theological students, pastors in training and church homegroups, this book is a transformative tool for those committed to cultivating a life of character and virtue.

Bennet Lawrence, PhD
Regional Secretary, ATA India

There is a lot of great literature for Christians to read about character development. What is less common is a resource that helps the church and individuals put theory into practice. That is exactly what this workbook does. In an accessible, easy-to-grasp format, the *Character and Virtue in Practice* workbook delivers on what it promises; to lead individuals, churches, students and teams through a process of deeper discipleship and spiritual formation.

Connie Main Duarte
Co-General Secretary, European Evangelical Alliance

This is an engaging and well-written manual with sound biblical teaching and a down-to-earth practice, laid out in a user-friendly format. Marvin has given us a fresh perspective on Christian life formation by directing us through twenty-four weeks of character and virtue education. Indeed, "virtue is a common heritage of humanity" (p45). It is my hope that the workbook will be made available to the non-English speaking community.

Michael Phua
Academic Dean,
Italian Chinese Theological Seminary, Italy

Sadly, a few pastors in the non-formal sector resort to an unfortunate expediency in their day-to-day pastoral praxis, characterized by a lack of integrity. This workbook by Marvin Oxenham makes a helpful contribution towards solving that problem. Those who diligently work through the exercises will greatly benefit, as will their churches.

Reuben van Rensburg, PhD
Project Director, Re-Forma

When a person does not practice what they profess, it is not just a problem of what is believed, but also what is valued. And yet values are anchored deeper still by virtues. Marvin Oxenham facilitates a self-guided tour with a pedagogically excellent workbook on Christian character. This teacher-mentor leads any willing reader or group in exploring the necessary virtues that underpin the spiritual values that overflow into Christ-like behaviour. If you are seeking Christic in-formation built on reliable information, here is your workbook into biblical maturity.

Ramesh Richard, PhD, ThD
President, RREACH
Professor of Global Theological Engagement and Pastoral Ministries,
Dallas Theological Seminary, Texas, USA

Character and Virtue in Practice is an indispensable resource for educators, discipleship leaders and individual learners seeking to intentionally shape character with practical, research-based tools. Building on Dr. Oxenham's extensive research, this workbook bridges scholarship with everyday

application, making it ideal for both formal and non-formal theological education, as well as various formation contexts.

Barry Saylor, DMin
Executive Director,
World Alliance for Pentecostal Theological Education

In this results-oriented world, the call to focus on character and virtue is imperative. Too often the clamour is for people to be more competent. Dr. Oxenham points out that competency is rooted in character and educating your character in virtue is central to becoming competent in other areas. Defining virtue as the habit of being good allows for a deep exploration of how to be godly. The focus on character and virtue is just what is needed to bring those inordinately focused on results back to being preceding doing. The development of character and virtue will only result in good works for the glory of God. I fully recommend this workbook.

Henry Tan, PhD
President, International Leadership Consortium – Cru

Testimonials

Here is what those who have worked through this plan to educate character and virtue have said . . .

I found this training plan to be well organized and structured, and it guided me week by week in diving deeper into knowing myself. Highly recommended!

This is not the usual personal growth course. It will help you to grasp a different perspective on who you are, and it will help you see exactly what you can work on in your character.

This plan helped me discover things about myself and the people around me that still help me on a daily basis.

Over these weeks I have seen great improvement in my exercise of virtue. I am really satisfied with my journey.

This journey has opened my eyes and I believe I have tackled the root of some problems in my character.

Overall, I am very pleased with this plan that has helped me work on virtue in my character. I definitely plan to continue to apply what I have learned to continue growing in virtue throughout my life.

I have seen the massive difference this kind of intentional plan has made.

This project has transformed my life and encouraged me to constantly engage in character self-assessment.

After the first few weeks of habituation I already began to actually feel good. And the more I practiced the plan, the more positive I have felt.

After I began to follow this plan, my personal mentor told me that I looked so much "freer" as if I had gained a new perspective!

If you can follow the plan in a small group that is ideal.

Being accountable in this journey was, in fact, the most challenging aspect, and yet the best part. It was great to strategize together on finding solutions and then share how things had gone over the week.

I was greatly helped by being part of a group of people who habituated virtue with me.

The experience of initially completing the Virtue Test was truly fascinating. At the end of the plan I took the Virtue Test again and it indicted significant growth in my character. These results absolutely reflect my own perception of growth over this journey.

Consistency and perseverance were the two big keys to completing this journey.

Others are noticing a change in my expression as a result of practising the virtue of magnanimity, and they are seeing real growth in my character as well as change in my prudence.

This journey into virtue has been a journey into self-awareness. I feel I have habituated my chosen virtue of truthfulness, and I am sure this will be a continuous task.

Interestingly, although I have particularly focused on growth in one virtue, I notice that I have been working subconsciously on other virtues as well, which I did not expect to happen.

The experience of self-assessment and habituation of virtue have greatly assisted me to take a step back, look in the mirror and reflect on who I am before God and before my fellow people.

ICETE Series

Character and Virtue in Practice

ICETE

Global Hub for Evangelical Theological Education

Langham

GLOBAL LIBRARY

Character and Virtue in Practice

A Workbook for Discipleship and Formation

Marvin Oxenham

Global Hub for Evangelical Theological Education

GLOBAL LIBRARY

© 2025 Marvin Oxenham

Published 2025 by Langham Global Library
An imprint of Langham Publishing
www.langhampublishing.org

Langham Publishing and its imprints are a ministry of Langham Partnership

Langham Partnership
PO Box 296, Carlisle, Cumbria, CA3 9WZ, UK
www.langham.org

ISBNs:
978-1-78641-051-1 Print
978-1-78641-104-4 ePub
978-1-78641-105-1 PDF

British Library Cataloguing-in-Publication Data
A catalogue record for this book is available from the British Library

ISBN: 978-1-78641-051-1

Cover & Book Design: projectluz.com

Contents

Preface xv

Introduction 1

Week 1   Why Character, What Virtue? 7

Week 2   About Virtue and Character 17

Week 3   Exploring Biblical Roots 29

Week 4   Virtue in Your Culture 41

Week 5   Making a Commitment 51

Week 6   Take the Virtue Test 61

Week 7   Interpreting the Virtue Test 67

Week 8   A Plan for Practice 77

Week 9   What Is Habituation 85

Week 10 Planning for Virtue 95

Week 11 Character Friendship 103

Week 12 Engage a Friend 111

Week 13 Improve Your Virtue Literacy 121

Week 14 Being Humble 131

Week 15 Being Temperate 141

Week 16 Being Courageous 151

Week 17 Being Just 161

Week 18 Being Compassionate 171

Week 19 Being Diligent 181

Week 20 Being Grateful 191

Week 21 Being Passionate 201

Week 22 Being Loving, Faithful and Hopeful 209

Week 23 Being Prudent 219

Week 24 Evaluate, Reflect and Celebrate 229

                  Group Facilitator Guidelines 243

                  Further Exploration 293

                  Notes 295

Preface

The cover of this workbook depicts Michelangelo's statue of David, wonderfully capturing the moment that precedes David's encounter with Goliath, as he firmly clutches his armed sling and gazes at the challenge before him.

This was a moment of great virtue in David's life. It was a moment of *faith* as he looked to God for the impossible. It was a moment of *hope* as he envisioned victory beyond defeat. It was a moment of *love* as he risked his life to stand in the gap for his community. But it was also a moment of *prudence* in the careful selection of weapons, a moment of *justice* in righting the wrongs of oppression, a moment of *courage* in standing firm despite his legitimate feelings of fear and a moment of quiet *self-control* in taming his will to do what was right.

But none of these virtues came to David suddenly in the moment that he stood before Goliath. Crisis moments, in fact, are moments of demonstration and not of development. The slow development of virtue had already taken place in David's life over time, through the slow discipline of becoming an accomplished musician, through the ongoing obedience to his father in menial duties, through the day-to-day duties of care and protection of his sheep, through the experiences of faith and courage in facing lions and bears in the lonely wilderness and through the regular reflection on the history of God and his work with Israel. These slow habits had slowly forged David's character with virtue. And these virtues were the "heart" of what God had seen when Samuel anointed him in Bethlehem.

It was this character of virtue, not his armour or ability, that equipped David for the moment of challenge.

The same is true for you. The key to a flourishing life of discipleship is virtue. Virtuous character will equip you to encounter the challenges of life. If want to glorify God with your life, what counts is the transformation of your character into the likeness of Christ's virtue.

But this transformation takes time and deliberate intention. And that is what this workbook is designed for.

Preface

The cover of this workbook depicts Michelangelo's statue of David, wonderfully capturing the moment that precedes David's encounter with Goliath, as he firmly clutches his armed sling and gazes at the challenge before him.

This was a moment of great virtue in David's life. It was a moment of *faith* as he looked to God for the impossible. It was a moment of *hope* as he envisioned victory beyond defeat. It was a moment of *love* as he risked his life to stand in the gap for his community. But it was also a moment of *prudence* in the careful selection of weapons, a moment of *justice* in righting the wrongs of oppression, a moment of *courage* in standing firm despite his legitimate feelings of fear and a moment of quiet *self-control* in taming his will to do what was right.

But none of these virtues came to David suddenly in the moment that he stood before Goliath. Crisis moments, in fact, are moments of demonstration and not of development. The slow development of virtue had already taken place in David's life over time, through the slow discipline of becoming an accomplished musician, through the ongoing obedience to his father in menial duties, through the day-to-day duties of care and protection of his sheep, through the experiences of faith and courage in facing lions and bears in the lonely wilderness and through the regular reflection on the history of God and his work with Israel. These slow habits had slowly forged David's character with virtue. And these virtues were the "heart" of what God had seen when Samuel anointed him in Bethlehem.

It was this character of virtue, not his armour or ability, that equipped David for the moment of challenge.

The same is true for you. The key to a flourishing life of discipleship is virtue. Virtuous character will equip you to encounter the challenges of life. If want to glorify God with your life, what counts is the transformation of your character into the likeness of Christ's virtue.

But this transformation takes time and deliberate intention. And that is what this workbook is designed for.

Introduction

Understand what this workbook is and how it works

A Training Workbook

My first book *Character and Virtue in Theological Education* had the intent of fuelling a new conversation around character and virtue in Christian formation. Although it was rich in practical ideas, I realized that a complementary workbook was needed that could easily be followed by individuals and communities wanting to grow in character and virtue.[1]

This workbook contains a twenty-four-week practice plan to educate your character according to virtue. It is not a book to read, but a training manual that you should follow. As you progress, in fact, you will regularly find places where you will be asked to respond, write your reflections, and journal on your growth. So always keep a pen with you!

Growth in character and virtue takes time, and the slow pacing of the activities in this workbook is meant to give you time to grow. None of the practices are complicated or long in themselves, but they need to be performed over a long time to be effective. You could read the workbook in a few hours and gain some interesting information, but you would miss out on the formation that is meant to happen over time. So, prepare to go slow.

Who Is It For?

This workbook applies consolidated practices of character education to Christian discipleship. It is hence written for a wide range of users that include both new Christians and seasoned believers, church members across a range of denominations, leaders involved in non-formal training programmes, theology students enrolled in formal programmes, missionary training and/or church planter training programmes, secondary school students in Christian schools, and any Christian individual or group that wants to engage intentionally with character growth.

Although the plan can work well as a personal activity, it works best when done in community. A theological school, for example, might adopt this workbook as the basis for a credit-bearing course in its curriculum. Or a rural training programme for pastors might use it to help young leaders grow in their character. Or again, a local church might use it as a mid-week house group meeting.

The workbook is designed to operate across global contexts and cultures. As an Italian author you will find that I often make references to the classical tradition of character and virtue with which I am most familiar, but throughout the workbook I will often encourage you to contextualize and seek out your own local traditions.

Planning and Scheduling

How then does it all work?

Each week you will be given about forty-five minutes of personal work, which include an introduction to the topic, a brief test to consolidate understanding, a concrete action point, a Bible study and a suggested prayer.

If you are working on character and virtue growth in a community setting, you will also normally engage in a group meeting. For facilitators leading these groups, weekly guidelines are provided in the Group Facilitator Guidelines in the final part of the workbook.

The schedule of this workbook has different stages:

- In the first stage (Weeks 1–5) you will understand what character and virtue education is, how it works, why it is important and where it is rooted.
- You will then engage in a self-evaluation stage (Weeks 6 and 7) where you will take a Virtue Test, evaluate your character and identify specific virtues in which you would like to grow.
- The longest stage (Weeks 8–23) centres around an intensive practice plan that applies the tools of habituation, character friendship and virtue literacy to help you grow in one selected virtue. Whereas the first two stages might be completed in less than 7 weeks, it is essential that you allow 15 weeks to complete this stage in order to benefit from the gradual effect of these practices.

- The plan concludes (Week 24) with an evaluation, an opportunity for in depth reflection on your growth and a time to celebrate and consider new plans.

These stages are designed to be consecutive, and the plan is meant to be completed over twenty-four consecutive weeks. If, for example, you begin the plan in September you should end sometime in February of the following year. This kind of scheduling should work well for individual users, local churches that have regular mid-week meetings, and for formal theological institutions that have weekly course timetables.

It is, however, possible to adapt the plan to different scheduling needs. For example, a group might organize two weekend retreats to cover the first and second stages in Weeks 1–7, followed by 15 weeks of independent work to complete the activities in Weeks 8–23, and concluding with a second retreat dealing with the activities outlined in Week 24. The plan can also be delivered in part or entirely with the support of online tools. These alternative schedules might work better for non-formal training programmes, for international networks that have difficulties in meeting face-to-face or for formal institutions offering online or hybrid programmes.

If alternative scheduling is used, it is important to respect the consecutive nature of the plan and to maintain the overall time to complete it, which should never be less than five to six months, in order to allow growth to happen gradually (the plan will not work as an intensive course).

Throughout the workbook you will find QR codes that are linked to the website www.virtueducation.net that was the original source of these materials.[2] The QR codes give you access to additional resources, charts, images and to interactive functions like the Virtue Test.

In the Further Exploration section at the end of the workbook you will find a QR code leading to a webpage with a wealth of continually updated materials related to the weekly topics. It is advised to visit these pages regularly.

Verify

Now take a few moments to verify your understanding of what this workbook is and how it works.[3]

(a) This workbook is not a book to read but a training manual.   ❏ True   ❏ False

(b) Growth in character and virtue takes _____ so I must prepare to go

_____.

(c) This workbook is designed specifically for a wide range of Christian disciples.   ❏ True   ❏ False

(d) The growth plan works well for personal devotions but works best in a community.   ❏ True   ❏ False

(e) Each week features about forty-five minutes of activities, plus an optional group meeting of about one hour.   ❏ True   ❏ False

(f) The plan is meant to be completed over twenty-four consecutive weeks, but the scheduling can be adapted as long as the overall time frame is never less than five to six months.   ❏ True   ❏ False

Ready for the Journey?

There are many metaphors in the Bible that describe growth and transformation. But the metaphor of the journey is probably one of the most popular.

Abraham journeyed to the promised land. Israel was called on a journey from slavery in Egypt to the promised land. Nehemiah journeyed to Jerusalem to build a wall. Jesus walked over 5,000 kilometres which amounts to around 1,000 hours of walking (about 15 percent of Jesus's three years of public ministry were spent walking). And the disciples were called to walk with him on a slow journey of growth.

This workbook invites you to a slow journey of growth in character and virtue. Are you ready?

Week 1

Why Character, What Virtue?

Start your journey of discipleship into virtue here

This workbook is meant to lead you through a practical plan to nourish virtuous character. Its core objective is not to *inform* you but to help *form* your character according to virtue.

In this first lesson, you will learn why character is important in your walk of discipleship and what being transformed by virtue might look like.

Why Character Is Important

As you set out on this transforming journey of discipleship, start with the "why" question. Why should you give time to this? Here are five interrelated reasons meant to motivate and inspire you in the months to come as you invest in character and virtue education.

N.1 – You will glorify God. Character and virtue education can be considered a trinitarian pathway to glorify God the Father, follow the Son and collaborate with the Holy Spirit.

You may have never thought about this. God designed you for virtue, Jesus called you to imitate his virtuous character and the Holy Spirit indwells you to produce the virtues of *love, joy, peace, patience, kindness, goodness, faithfulness, gentleness* and *self-control*. So, as you become more virtuous, you are fulfilling the purpose for which you were created, you are following in Jesus's footsteps, and you are collaborating with the transformative power of the Holy Spirit.

N.2 – You will deepen your walk of discipleship. A second reason to invest in character and virtue education is that it will impact your walk as a disciple. There are many different approaches to discipleship. Some focus on Christian service, others on biblical knowledge, others yet on deepening your devotional life or on helping you become a more effective leader.

Character and virtue education has the distinctive focus on developing who you *are*. Rather than focusing on the areas of knowing and doing, character and virtue discipleship intentionally develops the area of *being*. The New Testament expresses this in many ways: offering ourselves in holy sacrifice (Rom 12:1), walking in a manner worthy of the gospel (Phil 1:27), putting your earthly nature to death (Col 3:5), walking by the Spirit (Gal 5:16), being holy in all you do (1 Pet 1:16) and adding virtue to your faith (2 Pet 1:15).

N.3 – You will flourish. A third connected result of virtue education is that, in becoming a better person, you will flourish as a human being and attain a deep sense of peace, fulfilment and mature happiness that transcends your circumstances.

Flourishing is, in fact, connected to goodness. If you are a good person, you will flourish even when life is difficult. If, instead, you are a bad person, you will never truly flourish, no matter how favourable your circumstances may be.

This is because you are designed for virtue, and when you develop virtue, you become what you are meant to be. Another way of saying this is you flourish as you become genuinely you.

N.4 – You will perform better. Another great result of character and virtue education is that you will ultimately perform better. When you are a better person, you will normally do things better and achieve better results. Being more *courageous* will make you a better entrepreneur. Being more *compassionate* will make you a better leader. Being more *patient* will make you a better father. Being more *self-controlled* will help you collaborate better with others.

There is a lot of focus on competencies today, and we should not make the mistake of thinking that competencies have to do mostly with technique. Competencies are rooted in character and as you focus on educating your character in virtue, you will improve in many competences as well.

N.5 – You will improve the world around you. A final benefit of character and virtue education concerns those around you. Where virtue prospers in a community, the community is healthy. Where instead vice succeeds, the community falls apart.

This is true at all levels. At the most intimate level, shared virtue strongly binds friendships and marriages. Virtue also impacts neighbourhoods, churches, families, work environments and schools, that flourish as their members exhibit virtues and become dysfunctional as their members yield to vice. Leaders of these communities have a great responsibility to cultivate their own character. When they are loving, generous and passionate, their communities thrive. When they are proud, greedy or power-hungry, their communities flounder, no matter how orthodox their teaching is or how efficient they are in organizational matters.

We can also see the benefits of virtue in society at large. Good societies have citizens that are just, self-controlled, wise and courageous. Sadly, history also has many accounts of societies where the vices have taken over and led to their decadence.

Hopefully theses five motivations for engaging in this project of character and virtue education will inspire you. You have before you an opportunity to glorify God, deepen your walk of discipleship, become a better flourishing person, improve your competences, and bless your relationships and the communities of which you are a part. Considering all this, working on your character and improving your virtue may well be one of the most important investments of your life.

What Virtue Looks Like

Let us now move to the "what" question. What might more virtue in your character look like? What can you expect of this project for you? The following imaginary story about Beatrice introduces some answers to these questions.

Beatrice's friends knew her as a selfish person and a crazy driver. Behind the wheel, she made illegal U-turns, did not respect pedestrian crossings and had little regard for speed limits. This reflected her attitude towards in life in general, where she thought mostly of herself, bending rules and generally disregarding those around her.

When Beatrice began to work on her character in her church discipleship group, her attention was soon drawn to the fact that her behaviour behind the wheel demonstrated a lack of a particular virtue. To her surprise, she discovered that the name of this virtue was *justice*. She learned that justice has to do with respecting the rights of others as opposed to living only for one's self-interests. She realized that, as she drove, she was not thinking about others, but only about herself, about her schedule, about her being annoyed with traffic and with slow drivers.

So she put her will to action and made a commitment to intentionally cultivate justice in her character by replacing bad driving habits with good ones. As a first step, she placed a small sign on the dashboard of her car that read "Driven by Justice."

Initially it was difficult, and the bad habits continued to prevail. But, as the months passed, Beatrice forced herself to obey traffic rules and to make herself accountable to her weekly discipleship group. She also prayed daily that God would help her to be a woman of true justice and began a small group Bible study on justice for her personal devotions. Gradually, she began to feel good about her new driving attitude and she experienced healthy satisfaction in her own virtuous behaviour. Occasionally she would run the odd red light but would feel bad about it. Once, after doing so, she stopped at the other side of the intersection, watched the light turn green, then turn red, and then turn green again. Only then did she continue her journey with a prayer and renewed determination.

Over time, as she put into practice the character education tools that she was learning about, it became more natural to act with justice. The temptations of impatience diminished, and the desires to break rules were replaced by desires to respect others.

After about six months her reputation changed. Not only did others perceive her as a safe driver but they also noted a generic change in her character. Her closest friends noted that she was much less selfish, much more concerned about others around her and generally a much nicer person to be around.

Something deep and lasting had taken place in her life. Her character had changed to be more virtuous.

Marks of Character Growth

The story of Beatrice illustrates five marks of genuine growth in character that you can hope to achieve as you follow the guidelines that are found in this workbook (note, these are not necessarily chronological).[4]

1. Virtue will shape your attention. This means that you will increasingly notice and attend to situations that require specific virtues. In the case of Beatrice, she noticed how her driving habits needed to be shaped by the virtue of *justice*. Her attention focused on specific vices that were standing in the way of justice, and in particular the vices of *impatience, selfishness,* and lack of *self-control*. As you grow in virtue, you will not only judge things differently and develop a new vocabulary around virtue, but you will also experience new levels of discernment and sensitivity related to virtue.

2. Virtue will bend your will to action. This means that you will make decisions to act in ways that are virtuous. Beatrice decided to change her driving habits and apply principles of virtue education to her life. This can be initially very difficult. Your will might not bend easily, because you are choosing actions that go in a different direction than what you are used to. It will be like straightening a crooked rod that initially requires much pressure. But, as you saw in Beatrice, the more you act on your will, the easier it becomes. As you grow in virtue, you will increasingly welcome experiences that will allow you to practice your commitment.

3. Virtue will change your emotions. As she worked on her habits, Beatrice began to "feel good" about doing the right thing and "feeling bad" about breaking rules. This is a powerful dynamic. As you repeat virtue-related actions, you will experience good feelings that are roused by virtue, and you will experience bad feelings in the presence of vice. As your character changes and you increasingly become a virtuous person, you can anticipate feeling a deep sense of happiness and attraction to what is good.

4. Virtue will determine your desires. As you practice virtue you will increasingly want to see changes in your character for the good. Whereas initially your will is more active in cultivating virtue, as you progress, your desires will motivate you to do what is good. Beatrice began with a choice of the will, but as her character began to change, she found herself attracted to virtue. If temptation can be defined as being torn between the desires of virtue and vice, you can anticipate that educating your character towards virtue will lessen the forces of temptation.

5. Virtue will influence your expression. This is how others perceive you. Initially, Beatrice's friends perceived her as a crazy driver, but even more significantly they perceived her as being selfish. As Beatrice changed, those around her perceived her as someone who was respectful of others. The same can happen to you as you develop character.

Changing your attention, actions, emotions, desires and expression are fantastic outcomes. But they do not come easily. As with all worthwhile things, there is a price to pay. Growth in character is not something that happens overnight. This workbook is designed to help you invest twenty-four weeks in working through a set of practices.

In the beginning it will be difficult, and it will require the continual exercise of your conscious will. But in time, you will begin to experience virtue as a natural part of your character.

If this is what you want, press on. This character growth project is for you!

Verify

Respond now to some brief questions to ensure your understanding and to reinforce your memory of the main points. Write your answers in the spaces below.[5]

(a) The main purpose of this workbook is not to inform you but to _____ you.

(b) Virtue education assumes that happiness is connected to _____.

(c) Competences without character can be mere techniques that may not stand the tests of real life.   ❑ True   ❑ False

(d) Dysfunctional communities are usually rooted in the _____ of its members.

(e) When you increasingly notice situations that require virtue, your _____ is being shaped.

(f) When you increasingly make conscious decisions to act virtuously, your _____ is being shaped.

(g) When you increasingly feel good about doing the right things, your _____ is being shaped.

(h) When you want to see more changes in your character for the good, your _____ is being shaped.

(i) When others increasingly perceive you as virtuous, your _____ is being shaped.

Act: Write Your Motivations

Each week, this section of the workbook will suggest a small action point. This first week consists in a simple writing exercise about your motivation. You have seen five motivations meant to inspire you to seek to educate your character according to virtue.

- You will glorify God, follow Jesus and cooperate with the Spirit
- You will deepen your walk as a Christian disciple
- You will flourish
- You will perform better
- You will improve the world around you

Rewrite these motivations in your own words in the order in which they inspire you most. Begin each sentence with the words "I want to . . ."

† Bible Study: The New Self

Read: Colossians 3:1–14

Each week you will find a brief Bible study that relates to the topic of the week. This week you will see how Colossians 3 relates to the "why" and the "what" of character and virtue education.

The book of Colossians contains a strong message about virtue. Right from the first chapter we are instructed about living a life worthy of the Lord and of pleasing him in every way (Col 1:10). These are inspiring words, but what do they mean in practice? How do we actually do this?

Paul's reply is found in the second part of this verse (Col 1:10–11). He tells us that we should bear fruit in _____ (fill in the blank) as we are strengthened with supernatural _____ (fill in the blank) from God (Col 1:10–11). But what are these good works?

As we come to chapter 3, Paul tells us what these good works are. And he does so by giving us a detailed list of the "things above" ("things" which we might also call "heavenly virtues") that are in contrast with the "earthly vices." Complete the table below, seeing if you can list the seven virtues in this chapter:

Seven heavenly virtues with which we are to clothe ourselves (3:12–14)

1) _____

2) _____

3) _____

4) _____

5) _____

6) _____

7) _____

Can you see that living a life worthy of the Lord and pleasing him in every way has to do with bearing the good fruit of virtue in your life?

Conclude by reading Colossians 3:10. This verse beautifully sums up the main points of this lesson. Why should you grow in character? Because this is how you reflect the image of your Creator. What does growth in virtue look like? It is putting on a new self of virtuous living, starting from love, which binds all virtues together in perfect unity (3:14).

Now respond: Look at the text in Colossians 3 again. Is there one vice in particular that you feel you need to put to death? Write it down in the box below. Is there one virtue that you know is weak in your life? Also write it down in the box below.

A Prayer

Oh Lord, as I start out on this journey of character and virtue education, I ask that by the power of your Spirit, you will fill me so that I may live a life worthy of you, pleasing you in every way, and bearing fruit in every good work of virtue.

In this first week you have considered why character and virtue are important and how you can expect to change. Next week you will understand better what virtue and character are and what it means to educate your character.

Date completed: _____

Week 2

About Virtue and Character

Understand what we mean by virtue and character education

Although you may be anxious to begin the practical part of educating your character in virtue, you first need to gain some basic understanding. For, although knowing *about* virtue is not the same thing as *becoming* virtuous, it is the starting point. The first few weeks of this character growth project will, accordingly, offer a little more content. Later on, you will focus more on practice.

So let us start with some basic questions. What do we mean by virtue? How is it related to character? And what do we mean by educating our character in virtue?

What Is Virtue?

The word "virtue" is a beautiful word that has sadly slipped out of our contemporary vocabulary. Even in Christian circles, we often avoid the word "virtue" in favour of more generic terms like "values" or "integrity." And yet, virtue is a wonderful word with rich cultural and theological traditions, and to not use it is to do damage to ourselves.

Here is a nice, rich definition of virtue:

> *Virtues are stable dispositional clusters concerned with praiseworthy functioning in a number of significant and distinctive spheres of human life*[6]

The definition may seem a little complex at first, but it tells us several simple things. First, we see that virtues have to do with praiseworthy functioning.

So any of the functions in your life that are admirable are likely to be virtues. Second, we see that virtues are dispositions that make us act, think and feel in certain ways. So virtues are not theoretical concepts alone, but powerful forces that are at work in us. Third, virtues come in clusters and shape our character in ways that often overlap. Although we will often be thinking of individual virtues during this growth project, you need to remember that they are all interrelated. And finally, the definition reminds us that virtues are stable dispositions, meaning that they are not just occasional occurrences of good deeds, but that they are embedded into our character as something permanent.

How about a simpler definition? Here is one that summarises what many scholars have written about:

> *Virtue is the habit of being good.*

This definition suggests that virtue is fundamentally a habit. It is a habit that defines who we are. Since it is a habit that revolves around goodness, virtue is what makes us good people. The opposite of virtue is vice, which is the habit of being bad and which makes us bad people.

Although we do not always find the exact words "virtue" and "vice" in the Bible, the concepts that we have just described are very biblical. The Old Testament, for example, speaks of "holiness" to describe the good character of God's people. The New Testament, instead, uses the Greek word for virtue *arete*,[7] and many other synonyms for being good people such as "righteousness," and "sanctification."

The Bible also has many examples of vice, most frequently referred to as "sin," as that which falls short of virtue and of the perfect moral character of God. Theologians like Thomas Aquinas, have made direct connections between vice and sin, suggesting, for example, that the seven capital vices of *pride, envy, wrath, sloth/acedia, avarice, gluttony* and *lust* are the source of all sin.

In addition to thinking about virtue as a general concept, you can also think about the virtues (in the plural). They can, in fact, be listed, organized and classified in ways that give a fuller understanding of what virtuous character looks like.

Take a few minutes now to look at the Virtue Wheel below.

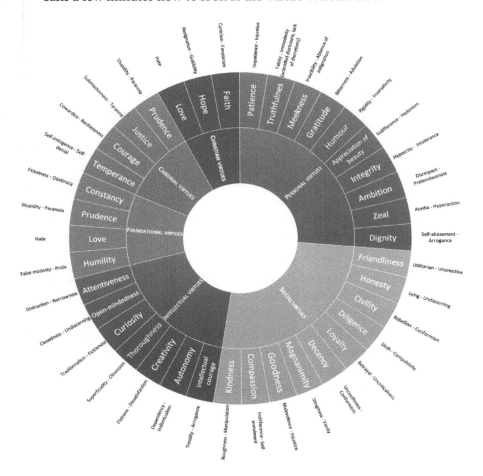

Scan the QR code to download a high-resolution file of the Virtue Wheel.

(The Virtue Wheel)[8]

Notice a few things. As you can see, the inner part of the Virtue Wheel suggests six possible categories for the virtues, including Cardinal, Foundational, Theological, Social, Personal and Intellectual virtues. In the second circle you can see examples of the virtues in each category.

- The Cardinal virtues include *prudence, justice, temperance* and *courage.*
- The Foundational virtues include *constancy* and *humility.*
- The Theological virtues include *faith, hope* and *love.*
- The Social virtues include *kindness, compassion, decency, loyalty, diligence, honesty* and *friendliness.*
- The Personal virtues include *zeal, dignity, integrity, ambition, gratitude* and *humour.*
- The Intellectual virtues include *attentiveness, creativity, curiosity* and *open-mindedness.*

For each virtue, the Virtue Wheel also offers examples of the vices-by-excess and vices-by-defect of each virtue. These are found in the outer circle. We will come back to these later on in this workbook.

Please note that the Virtue Wheel is only an example of a selection of virtues and how they might be organized. It is not exhaustive nor exclusive, and there are many different lists of virtues and many ways to organize them. As you begin your character growth project, however, these examples can begin to enrich your vocabulary around virtue.

What Is Character?

Now, let's move on to the second question. How is virtue related to character? And what do we even mean by character?

A first issue is the actual word character, because it may translate in different contexts and languages to mean several things.

In English, for example, it is often used to describe personality traits, such as being introverts or extroverts. But that is not what we mean here. When we speak about character in the context of character and virtue education, we are talking about being a good or bad person, and not about morally neutral traits of our personality. So, for example, being an extrovert is morally neutral. Being proud, instead has moral implications. That is why extroversion is a matter of personality, whereas pride is a matter of character.

Imagine your character as your moral DNA. Do you recall the story of Beatrice from last week? In a way, her character was missing a piece of moral DNA related to the virtue of justice. Her character also contained some flawed code around the vice of selfishness. This moral DNA influenced her actions, her feelings, her desires and the ways that others perceived her. Character growth required changing her moral DNA. This is what the education of character does.

Why Education?

This workbook will often use the following three words together: "character and virtue education." The word education is therefore a third important word to focus on. It is important because it indicates an intentional process to change something for the better. In this case, it is about changing your character to become more virtuous.

We could use many other words that are similar to education, like training, growing, cultivating, mentoring, facilitating or discipling. But education is a rich word, and we should not discard it. It comes from the Latin *educere*, which has the idea of "leading us to become better." Can you imagine a better way to describe character and virtue education than being led to become a better person?

As a Christian you may wonder how education relates to the work of God in your life. Does education and the emphasis on human action not detract from the work of God? Should we not simply pray and wait for God to do his work in us?

This passive/receptive approach to discipleship is surely meant to honour the sovereignty of God. But it is wrong, for the simple fact that God himself calls us to collaborate with him and actively cooperate with him in educating our character. There is a mysterious interplay in discipleship where both God and the disciple are actively involved. It is not "*either* God or you," but "*both* God *and* you." Jesus called, *and* the disciples followed. Jesus taught, *and* the disciples decided to obey. Jesus healed, *and* the healed had faith *and* they took initiative to travel to where Jesus was. God made the seeds grow, *and* Paul planted, *and* Apollos watered. And so with you. God is at work in you to shape your character in his image, *and* you are called to educate your character in virtue using all the tools that are available.

Think of sailing. In order for a sailboat to move two things must happen. First, the sails need to be raised. Second, the wind needs to blow. Without one of these two things, the boat will not move. A sail with no wind gets us nowhere.

Likewise, if wind does not find a raised sail, it will blow over and produce no movement. So it is with God's work in you. As you make the intentional character education efforts suggested in this workbook you are raising your sail. But you need to look to God to blow his wind on your life in order that you may move forward and be transformed.

That is why there is a suggested prayer at the end of each week in this workbook. These prayers are not mere liturgical embellishments to conclude a lesson, but represent genuine requests for God's transforming power in your character.

✅ Verify

Respond now to some brief questions to ensure your understanding and to reinforce your memory of the main points. Write your answers in the spaces below.[9]

(a) Write your definition of the word "virtue." _____
_____
_____

(b) What are some "biblical" concepts that are similar to the concepts of "virtue" and "vice"?
_____
_____

(c) There is only one complete list of virtues and only one way to classify the virtues that is valid for all times and cultures.   ❏ True ❏ False

(d) In what classification might the virtue of courage be placed? _____
_____

(e) In what classification might the virtue of curiosity be placed? _____
_____

(f) Write two virtues that might be classified as social virtues.

_____ and _____

(g) Write two virtues that you see as important in your culture and context.

_____ and _____

(h) What seven virtues might counter the seven capital vices? _____,

_____, _____, _____,

_____, _____, _____

(i) The metaphor used in this chapter to illustrate your cooperation with God in shaping your

character is _____.

(j) We can educate our character in virtue with no help needed from God.   ❑ True
                                                                                   ❑ False

(k) God will change our character to become more virtuous with intentional effort   ❑ True
   on our part.   ❑ False

 Act: Exploring Your Context

This workbook is meant to serve many contexts, cultures and languages and as you progress through the coming weeks, you should be continually thinking about your own culture and context. Here is a first opportunity to do so.

What are the words for "virtue," "character" and "education" in your language? Write them in the box below together with their definitions.

If English is your native language, complete the exercise looking for further definitions, synonyms, etymology and opposites of these words.

Bible Study: Add to Your Faith, Virtue

Read: 2 Peter 1:5

In the Bible study for this week, you will look at the importance of adding virtue to your walk of discipleship. If you have responded to God's calling into his kingdom, the most important thing in your life is now to add virtue to your faith. That is the message of the little letter of 2 Peter.

The letter was written in a peculiar historical context. It was a time in which discourse around virtue and vice was prevalent among Greek and Roman philosophers, poets and politicians. But it was also a time when, in practice, the vices were prevailing. In particular, the letter was probably written during the time of the emperor Nero who was known for killing his wives, burning Christians, poisoning his competitors and levelling most of Rome to build the fabulous Domus Aurea. He also induced his mentor Seneca, one of the greatest philosophers around virtue of all times, to commit suicide.

In the middle of all this, Peter reminds his Christian readers to "add to your faith, virtue."

There are three key expressions that we find in 2 Peter 1:5.

1. **Make every effort to add**. This is the central exhortation. It is an imperative verb that calls for a creative, committed, deep, sincere, sustained effort around virtue. It represents the moment when, as a disciple of Jesus, you quit blaming others for your weaknesses, you quit making excuses for your faults and you take ownership of your own character. It is when you tone down the God-loves-me-just-as-I-am dial and turn up your own responsibility dial.

    If we do not add virtue to live holy and godly lives, there are consequences. 2 Peter 3:2 warns us that we will be ineffective and unproductive, near-sighted and blind and that we will risk stumbling in our walk.

    So "just faith" is not enough if we seek a full Christian walk of discipleship. We must add virtue.

2. **Add virtue**. Virtue is the key word that is connected to the main exhortation. We must add virtue. The term for virtue (sometimes blandly translated as "goodness"), is the Greek word *arête*, which is the same word used by Socrates, Plato, Aristotle and many others as they wrote about the virtuous life. In the choice of this word we see the beginning of the strong connection that lasted centuries

between the classical tradition around virtue and Christian theology and practice (more of this next week).

You may also note that the call to add virtue to your faith is followed by an ethical list. The educated reader of the time would have immediately spotted the well-established classical categorization that begins with a list of private virtues (*knowledge, self-control, perseverance* and *godliness*) and is followed by a list of public virtues (*mutual affection* and *love*).

3. **Add through the divine power.** We are called to add virtue to our faith. But how can this be done? What hope was there for the readers of this letter to become virtuous, especially when society was so full of vice? This was the quest of the classical philosophers. How do you obtain *arête*? Is it through philosophy? Is it through practices of detachment from desire? Is it through education? Is it through a healthy *polis*? Is it through teaching ethical lists? All these things were good, but they were also lacking.

So here is the good news: "His divine power has given us everything we need for a godly life" (2 Pet 1:3). This is the good news of the gospel. The gospel is not just that we get to go to heaven, but also that we also get to be good people. God's divine power forgives our sins, but it also empowers us for a life of virtue.

Peter tells us that for anyone to be truly virtuous, divine power from above is needed.

Now respond: This text reminds you of your responsibility to add virtue to your faith. But it also reminds you that through Jesus you have received the power to do so. How does this teaching contribute to your understanding of your walk of discipleship? Write a few sentences in the box below to consolidate what this means for you.

🙏 A Prayer

Lord, I wish to add virtue to my faith so that I may be effective, clear sighted and not stumble. I commit to doing my part in adding virtue. I however ask that your divine power give me all that I need to live a godly life and thus confirm my calling and election.

> This week you have had a short introduction to some very deep
> issues on virtue, character and education and how they relate
> to your walk of discipleship. Next week you will look at the
> Christian and biblical roots of character and virtue education.

Date completed: _____

Week 3

Exploring Biblical Roots

Discover character and virtue education in the Bible and in the Christian tradition

You may have never heard about character and virtue education before, and you may be wondering if it something new. In this chapter you will look at examples from the Bible, from church history and from the Christian tradition to help you appreciate that character and virtue education represents a long-standing tradition in the Bible and in Christianity.

Roots in the Old Testament

Although virtue language is not always explicit in the Old Testament, its books are infused with a theology of virtue, with instructions around virtue and with examples of virtue. Consider some examples of each of these.

A theology of virtue. Let us start with a theology of character virtue rooted in the Genesis creation account. In chapters 1 and 2 we see that God made humans in his image and called humanity to live in accordance with this image. But what does the image of God entail? It entails many things, among which his moral character. God is love, so we are called to *love*. God is patient, so we should develop the virtue of *patience*. God is creative, so our character should reflect the virtue of *creativity*. And so on.

In Genesis 3 and 4 we read of the fall. But how did it happen? It happened through sin, which is a distortion of the virtuous pattern of living that God had intended for humanity. In particular, we see *faith* being replaced by *disobedience* and *ambition* (in Adam and Eve) and *humility* being replaced by *envy* and *anger* (in Cain). These sins might also be called vices as they debase the character of man and stain the original image of God. In Genesis 6 we find that the lack of virtue and the prevalence of *evil* and *violence* becomes so great, that God regrets making human beings.

The rest of the book of Genesis is the story of how God begins his work with the people of Israel, calling them to be people where the virtues of *justice*, *mercy* and *holiness* might be seen as a reflection of his own character.

Instructions around virtue. The Old Testament is also rich in instructions about what the virtuous life looks like. We have, for example, the Ten Commandments, which show us what it means to be *faithful*, *honest*, *temperate*, *humble*, *just*, *chaste*, *truthful* and not *greedy*. We have books like Deuteronomy, that are meant to educate a new generation in what it means to be *holy* and *just*.

We also have books of wisdom and poetry, that offer explicit teaching around character, such as the well-known tree metaphor in Psalm 1 that depicts the ways of the wicked and the ways of the righteous. The book of Proverbs in particular is a genuine manifesto of virtuous character. In it wisdom is closely associated with goodness and virtue, and we find repeated examples of viceful individuals who are called fools, and of virtuous women and men who are called wise (see, for example the "virtuous woman" in chapter 31).

Stories of virtue. In addition to a theology of virtue and instruction of virtue, the Old Testament is a treasure of stories of virtue. Imagine young children listening to their parents and grandparents on desert nights as they were told about the *prudence* of Joseph, the *wisdom* of Solomon, the *courage* of David, the *faith* of Abraham and the *hope* of Moses. But also, their character was shaped as they heard the negative stories of the *envy* of Cain, the *greed* of Haman or the *complacency* of old Eli.

These stories of virtue and vice from Israel's national history had a profound impact on the imagination of successive generations and created desires for emulation that had great educational value.

Roots in the New Testament

Jesus and virtue. As we come to the New Testament, we naturally start with Jesus. What can we learn from him about virtue and character? In general, we observe that Jesus developed the Old Testament tradition, calling his followers not only to the external observation of the law but to a radical inner change of character.

In the Gospels, we note that much of Jesus's teaching was concerned with character and virtues. His longest recorded sermon (the one "on the mount"), focuses on the virtues of *meekness*, of *love* of our neighbours (and enemies) and on the virtue of *hope*. It also denounces the vices of *hypocrisy*, *wrath*, *pride* and *greed*.

But Jesus did more than just teach about virtue. As we look at his ministry of discipleship, we see that he is intent on cultivating the character of his disciples. He was not just concerned with what they needed to know, nor with equipping them with what they needed to do. He had a passion to transform them into the men of virtue that they needed to be. And so he exposed them to tests of *courage*, scolded them for their lack of *faith*, involved them in works of *compassion*, modelled how to be *shrewd* as snakes and *innocent* as doves and built them up to be a community of *love*.

As he did so, Jesus himself stood out as an example of virtue, demonstrating *self-control* in the face of temptation, *compassion* in healing the sick, *justice* in paying taxes to the Romans, *courage* in cleansing the temple, *zeal* in scolding the Pharisees and *humility* in washing his disciple's feet.

New Testament stories of virtue. The New Testament also tells many stories about virtue and vice. Paul is surely an important figure, and we are explicitly called to imitate his many virtues from his life, which include *zeal*, *constancy*, *patience*, *endurance in difficulties*, *love* and *contentment*. We also find inspiration in the stories of the *discretion* of Joseph, the *courage* of John the Baptist, the *intellectual honesty* of Nicodemus, the *generosity* of Cornelius and the *open-mindedness* of the Bereans. When it comes to examples of bad character, there is also much to shape our character as we look at the *envy* of Herod, the *cowardice* of Peter, the *falsity* of Ananias and Sapphira or the *inconstancy* of Mark.

Virtue in the teaching epistles. Moving to the epistles, they are also "virtue rich." Did you know, for example, that the New Testament has twenty-two lists of virtues and vices? For example, the well-known "fruit of the Spirit" in Galatians 5 is a virtue list, in which we find the virtues of *love*, *joy*, *peace*, *forbearance*, *kindness*, *goodness*, *faithfulness*, *gentleness* and *self-control*.

Generally speaking, the authors of the epistles considered the work of Christ and the advent of the Holy Spirit as wonderful "good news" that made it possible to walk in newness of life and transformed character.

Philippians, for example, tells us to work out our salvation through the virtues of *civility*, *love* and *humility* and Colossians defines pleasing the Lord in terms embodying virtue. The book of James is the New Testament equivalent to the book of Proverbs as it offers a Christian manifesto of practical virtue. The "pastoral" letters to Timothy and Titus are also virtue rich, as they prescribe the virtues that are necessary to be a church leader and make it clear that certain vices, like being *quick-tempered, drunkard, violent* or *pursuing dishonest gain* will lead to downfall.

Although the writers of the New Testament never systematized a language of character and virtue, they regularly used the Greek words of their time that referred to virtue (for example, *arête, dikaiosune* and *phronesis*) and it is clear that they appreciated the culture of their time that had developed sophisticated approaches to character and virtue education.

Roots in Church History and Theology

One of the notable features of the first centuries of church history was the encounter between classical/Greek culture and Christianity around the theme of virtue.

As early as the third century we find many references to virtue in the writings of scholars like Origen. The cultivation of the virtuous life was also considered central in leadership training of early church leaders, and we find thriving examples of Christian movements that openly pursued character and virtue, like the Christian hermits living in the Egyptian desert (the so-called "desert fathers and mothers") who lived drawing close to God and teaching others how to flee vice and pursue virtue.

Moving into the Middle Ages, the dialogue around character and virtue prospered, generating refined theologies of virtue and character education, which began to be rephrased in terms of "spiritual formation." The list of Christian theologians who engaged with the topic of virtue is long, and includes Cassian, Ambrose, Augustine, St. Benedict, St. Francis, Abelard and, most notably, Thomas Aquinas.

For complex reasons we won't get into, around the time of the sixteenth century in Europe, there was a general decline in interest around the virtues. Some argue that the Reformation contributed to this decline, as the Protestant emphasis on faith and redemption confused virtue education with salvation by works.

Today we are witnessing a renewed interest in the tradition of character and virtue in Christianity. In the evangelical world, in particular, thinkers like Stanley Hauerwas and N. T. Wright are writing again on the topic, and many theological schools, missions and church denominations are raising questions about how to shape the character of virtuous kingdom leaders.

Verify

This week you have received a crash course on character and virtue in the Bible and in the Christian tradition. As you can see, the topic is vast, and you have only scratched the surface. Enough has been said, however, to establish character and virtue as very important Christian themes.

As you progress through this workbook you will find brief Bible studies about virtue at the end of each week. By the time you finish, you will have completed more than twenty specific studies around this important topic.

Respond now to some brief questions to ensure your understanding and to reinforce your memory of the main points. Write your answers in the spaces below.[10]

(a) What was one important way that the Jewish nation educated virtue in its youth?

_____

(b) The story of Cain is an example of which vice? _____

(c) In Psalm 1, a synonym for the word virtue is _____.

(d) The Old Testament book that is a "manifesto of virtuous character" is

_____.

(e) Give two examples of virtues that Jesus used in his teaching and discipleship.

_____,

_____

(f) There are at least twenty-two "ethical lists" of virtues and vices in the New Testament.

❑ True
❑ False

(g) Which New Testament books feature the virtues needed for church leaders?

_____, _____

(h) The New Testament uses Greek words commonly used by contemporary philosophers to talk about virtue.

❑ True
❑ False

(i) Name one of the church fathers who engaged with the tradition of character and virtue.

_____

(j) Interest in character and virtue has always been exactly the same in all of church history.

❑ True
❑ False

 Act: Start a Conversation

The action point for this week involves starting a conversation with other Christians around the topic of character and virtue. To do so, use the following brief survey with at least three people and record their answers.

(1) What is the first thing that comes to mind when you hear the word "virtue"?

(2) How important is character in Christian discipleship?

(3) Can you think of places in the Bible that talk about character and virtue?

📖 Bible Study: Ethical Lists in the New Testament

Read: key texts

The Bible study for this week gives you a closer look at the twenty-two lists of virtues and vices in the New Testament.

These so-called "ethical lists" represented a common device in classical literature as both Greek and Roman philosophers produced catalogues of specific virtues that were recommended or exemplified. These were very popular in ancient literature, and the New Testament contains twenty-two such lists, of which fourteen are lists of virtues and eight are lists of vices.

Example in Romans. In the book of Romans, you are probably familiar with the famous exhortation to offer ourselves as a "holy sacrifice" (Rom 12:1), but you may have never noticed that over the next four chapters Paul unfolds a list of virtues that help the reader understand in practice what "holy sacrifice" means.

For each verse below, match a corresponding virtue from the list:

13:5	_____
13:8	_____
13:13	_____
14:1	_____
14:21	_____
15:5	_____ and _____
15:13	_____
16:1	_____
16:17	_____
16:19	_____

List of virtues to match the verses above: civility, decency, tolerance, self-control, unselfishness, perseverance, knowledge, encouragement, generosity, watchfulness, wisdom, love, hope.

Seven ethical lists: Now engage with the following ethical lists of virtues. Read each text and write down the virtues that are listed.

Note: if you are working with a group, you may deal with these texts during your group meeting this week.

- Matthew 5–7 (what are the virtues in the Beatitudes?)

- Galatians 5:22–23 (notice that the "fruit of the Spirit" is a list of virtues)

- Colossians 3:12, 18–25 (the heading of this text is "excellence" which is the translation of *arete*, virtue)

- 1 Timothy 3; Titus 1 (what are the qualifications of virtuous leaders?)

- Mark 7 (notice that the "evils that come from inside" are vices)

- Romans 1:29–30 (the wickedness that brings judgement is a list of vices)

- 2 Corinthians 12 (here you will find the vices that can tear the church apart)

Now respond: What thoughts have stuck out as you engaged with these virtue lists in the New Testament?

A Prayer

Lord, as I present myself as a "holy sacrifice" to you, grant me your power to fulfil my commitment to humility, civility, service, teaching, encouragement, generosity, diligence, mercy, love, zeal, hope, patience, faith, solidarity, magnanimity, compassion, equity, justice and patience.

> This week you have had a brief introduction to the biblical and
> historical tradition concerning character and virtue in Christianity.
> Next week you will be exposed to some of the other global,
> philosophical and religious traditions around character and virtue.

Date completed: _____

Week 4

Virtue in Your Culture

Discover character and virtue education found in other cultures

Last week you were introduced to the tradition of character and virtue in Christianity. But what about other traditions and cultures? This week you will consider some examples of how the tradition of character and virtue is a recurring feature in global cultures, philosophies and religions.

You will look first at an example from an ancient culture, then at one from a world religion and from a philosopher and finally at some contemporary examples. We cannot consider examples from all cultures, but you will be given an opportunity to look for examples in your own culture and context.

As a result of this lesson you should be encouraged that as you engage in character and virtue education you are standing on the shoulders of giants and latching onto a global tradition that is acclaimed across history and culture.

Roots in Ancient Cultures

When looking for virtue traditions in the great ancient cultures of the world, the ancient Mesopotamian culture has been selected as an example because there is a great wealth of surviving literature in which virtue and character are a recurring motif. Here are some examples.

We can start with Sumerian praise literature, in which virtues are either explicitly praised or indirectly taught through the tale of heroes. Then we have codes and laws, like the famous Code of Hammurabi, which is meant to ensure *justice*, under the watchful eye of its divine guardian Marduk. The Mesopotamian myth genre also focuses on the virtues and vices and we find tales of the gods involved in *betrayal, friendship, loyalty, pride, jealousy, wrath,*

41

courage, lust, guile and *deceit.* This vision of the good and bad life is further reflected in the collections of wisdom literature that praise the person who is *prudent, obedient, learned, intelligent* and *religiously devout.*

Epics also have an important place in Mesopotamian literature, with the most famous likely being the Akkadian Epic of Gilgamesh. This story tells of the deeds of Gilgamesh, who offers sad examples of the vices of *impatience, egoism* and lack of *consideration of others*, but also shows us how to grow morally and learn how to accept mortality, grow in *courage* and enjoy what is good with *moderation.*

Roots in Confucianism

Let us now consider character and virtue in an ancient religion. Confucianism has been selected because there is much to be said about Confucius in relation to character and virtue. For him, the idea of *ren* as the "perfect virtue" (also translated as "benevolence," "goodness," or "humanness") was central. The main properties of *ren* are the virtues of *li* as propriety, *xiao* as filial piety, *ti* as brotherly love, *zhong* as loyalty, *shu* as tolerance, *yi* as righteousness, *zhi* as wisdom and *xin* as integrity.

For Confucius, *ren* is a quality that is available to all human beings and that can be cultivated and practised. It is not a special endowment for aristocrats or rulers alone but represents the potential of goodness in each human being. The outcome of virtue in Confucianism is human flourishing, defined as the state where human beings become more humanized as they grow in *ren*.

When it comes to education, the cultivation of *ren* is a primary objective in Confucianism which places high value on moral self-cultivation in communities of like-minded colleagues.

For Confucius, virtue is also particularly important for those who are in leadership positions. Confucius summarized the "five ways" of the virtuous leader as follows: "He is *reverent*, hence he receives no insults; he is *tolerant*, hence he gains the multitudes; he is *trustworthy*, hence others entrust him with responsibilities; he is *quick*, hence he has accomplishments; he is *generous*, hence he is capable of being placed in charge of others."[11] Embodiments of these high moral standards make a person fit to lead and to become a *junzi*: a gentleman or a morally ideal leader who will be able to transform society and make it well ordered.

Aristotelian Roots

We now turn to an example from the world of Greek philosophy, and in particular to Aristotle, whose contribution to the tradition of character and virtue is immense. Of all ancient Western thinkers, in fact, he is undoubtedly the highest authority in terms of virtue theories and practices.

Here are some highlights of what Aristotle said:

- Humanity has a purpose (*telos*), and that purpose is found in being agents of goodness and virtue.
- When humans fulfil their purpose, they find deep happiness (*eudaemonia*). Hence virtue is the road to human flourishing. In the *Nicomachean Ethics*, Aristotle claims that "human happiness is the activity of the soul in accordance with virtue."[12]
- The soul is always developing, either towards vice or towards virtue, and education is the force that will make the difference. Education of virtue should, therefore, be a central activity for all human communities.
- To educate virtue we need a holistic approach that includes reason, knowledge, emotions, the will and action.
- There is no one "bag of virtues" that can be prescribed for everyone at all times (maybe with the exception of the cardinal virtues). Individuals instead must be conscious that virtues take on different faces in different contexts and this means that wisdom (*prudence*) is the first virtue that will help us discern the best available good in any given circumstance.
- Virtue is often found in the middle between the extremes of defect and excess. So, the virtue of *courage* is the "golden mean" between the vices of *cowardice* (defect) and *excess* (recklessness). To grow in virtue, you must know whether you need to correct defect or excess.
- Virtue gradually becomes a natural part of our character through repetition. This is called habituation. You will learn more about this important practice later in this workbook.

Aristotle's framework for character and virtue education deeply influenced classical culture and early Christian theologians and is still today an important reference for anyone who is engaging in character education.

Contemporary Revivals

The three examples given above from Mesopotamian literature, Confucius and Aristotle may give you the impression that character and virtue education is something from the past. But it is not so. For there is today a vibrant renewed focus on virtue and character.

Here are some examples of general trends.

- Curricula of primary and secondary schools are being enriched by character and virtue education programmes and trends are beginning to appear in higher education as well.
- In Chinese culture, there is a return to the Confucian past to reshape present moral identity.
- In Western culture, there is a revival of Aristotelianism and a new interest in the virtues.
- In the academic world, there is a renewed interest in virtue ethics as a viable alternative to other ethical theories.
- Character and virtue are becoming popular today in the professional paradigms of law, health, media, business, professional workers, high finance, in the corporate management world and in the sciences. A growing body of research is being produced in these fields.
- Social and emotional learning (aka emotional-intelligence theory), communitarian brands of citizenship education and positive psychology's virtue theory, all claim to be informed by and seek inspiration from the thoughts of the ancient philosopher Aristotle.[13]
- In the field of religion and faith-based communities discourse around character and virtue is gaining traction, especially when it comes to leadership training.

Hopefully these tasters are enough to make you look closer into your own culture and context to see the roots and signs of character and virtue education.

Why the Overlaps with Christianity?

A question may linger in your mind as you compare what you've seen last week and this week. Last week you saw that character and virtue are part of the Christian tradition. And this week you have discovered that they are also part of other traditions. Why is this so?

The best explanation of this overlap is that virtue is a common heritage of humanity. If it is true that all humans are created in the image of God, it follows that everyone bears the imprint of his character and the aspiration to virtue. So although humanity has fallen from its original state and often gravitates towards sin and vice, this has not erased the memory nor the desire to cultivate virtue. If God has made humans for virtue, it is not surprising to discover that virtue is a universal quest.

As you consider committing to a plan of virtue education, it should be encouraging to know that this is not "just a Christian thing." Although there is a distinctiveness in the pursuit of virtue as a Christian, the pursuit of virtue is rooted in the fibre of humanity.

Verify

Verify what you have learned about the tradition of character and virtue in other cultures, religions and philosophies in the spaces below.[14]

(a) The tradition of character and virtue can be considered a common characteristic of humanity.   ❑ True   ❑ False

(b) List at least two kinds of ancient Mesopotamian literature that talk about virtue:

_____, _____

(c) What is the key word in Confucianism used to express virtue? _____

(d) What is the word for a morally ideal leader in Confucianism? _____

(e) Which philosopher has written more systematically about character and virtue than any other? _____

(f) For Aristotle, virtue is the road to human flourishing and happiness as we find the purpose of our being.   ❑ True   ❑ False

(g) Aristotle gave us a list of virtues that can be prescribed for everyone at all times.   ❑ True   ❑ False

(h) Aristotle deeply influenced Christian thinking about character and virtue.   ❑ True   ❑ False

(i) Revivals of interest in character and virtue are only found in Western religious circles.   ❑ True   ❑ False

Act: Look for Character and Virtue in Your Culture

This week you have seen some examples of the tradition of character and virtue in several world cultures. What about your context? Can you see a tradition of "character and virtue" in your culture?

Two weeks ago you did some research around the words for character and virtue in your language. The exercise for this week is to do a little more research into the traditions of character and virtue in your own culture. Keep in mind that the exact words "virtue and vice" may not be used in your culture, so look for similar concepts and practices (in Kenya, for example, the terms "discipline" and "indiscipline" are often used as synonyms for virtue and vice).

Try, for example, to write the word "virtue" and "your country" into your internet search engine (e.g. "virtue in Ghana" or "virtue in Peru"). Or try asking artificial intelligence (AI) about virtue in your own culture, about well-known texts in your tradition that talk about virtue, or about current practices in your context that focus on character education?

Although internet and AI will be a natural place to start, you might also want to entertain a conversation around these questions with elders in your community or perhaps do some research in a library.

Write what you find in the space below.

🕮 Bible Study: Wisdom and Virtue

Read: Proverbs (selected texts)

As you've seen, many different traditions are committed to the education of virtue. For the Jewish culture, this tradition is best expressed in the book of Proverbs.

Proverbs is the most explicit educational text of the Old Testament whose main concern is to educate in wisdom and goodness, both of which are closely associated with virtue.

It is practically impossible to read a single chapter of Proverbs without being impressed by the massive emphasis on character formation. Several general principles can be seen:[15]

1. God is the source of wisdom, and this wisdom is meant to shape the character of generation after generation.

2. The beginning of wisdom is the fear of the Lord, and the fulfilment of wisdom is a life of goodness and virtue.

3. Formation in the virtues is a communal activity in which those who are wiser have greater responsibilities towards the less mature.

4. Wisdom and the application of virtue concerns the whole of human experience, including work, rest, eating and speaking, each of which are put in relation to our character.

5. Character formation is an urgent matter. Choosing good or evil is a matter of life or death, and therefore education is an urgent matter.

Proverbs 2:7–11

Start by reading Proverbs 2:7–11 and make a few notes below on what it means to "turn your ear to wisdom."

As you have hopefully discovered, turning your ear to wisdom has to do with the virtues of being *upright, walking blamelessly* and *being right, just* and *fair*.

Also, you may have noticed that this passage has an emphasis on "being" and not just on mechanical obedience to a set of laws. Proverbs, in fact, is not meant to simply furnish a list of good things that we need to do and of bad things that we need to avoid. Wisdom is not mere prescription of outward behaviour. Rather, Proverbs continually points to the kind of people we should *be* and to the virtues that should shape our character.

Proverbs 8:13, 20
Read now Proverbs 8:13, 20 and make notes on what the opposite of wisdom looks like.

Have you noted that being a "fool" has to do with viceful character, *walking in dark ways, doing wrong* and *being perverted in evil*?

Proverbs 31 (optional)
If you want to read more, continue with Proverbs 31, and make a list of the virtues in the idealized portrait of the virtuous woman.

If you would like to undertake an even more ambitious project, read through the entire book of Proverbs and underline the virtues. At the very least, you will find that those who fear the Lord need to be *loving, trustworthy, humble, self-controlled, prudent, just, honest, kind, generous, truthful, gentle, patient, faithful, diligent, lovers of knowledge, zealous* and *moderate*. You will also find that, in order to avoid futility and punishment, we must not be *envious, lazy, false, proud, unjust, corrupt, lustful, violent, wrathful,* or *greedy*.

Now respond: Have you made the mistake of thinking that wisdom had to do with knowledge alone? Had you ever associated wisdom with being a good, virtuous person? What have you learned from the Bible study this week?

A Prayer

I come to you, God of the nations and source of all wisdom. I ask that my ear may be turned to wisdom that I may be upright, walk blamelessly and be just and fair.

This week you have appreciated the broader tradition of character and virtue and have begun to see it in your own culture. Next week concludes this first stage that has focused on understanding with a call to make a personal commitment to grow in character and virtue.

Date completed: _____

Week 5

Making a Commitment

Commit yourself to a journey of developing your character

After the first weeks of working through this workbook you should have a clearer idea about character and virtue education and how it is an important component in your walk as a disciple of Jesus.

You have also seen that you are not alone in this journey and that you are engaging with a historical tradition that is shared by humanity across ages, cultures, philosophies and religions.

Now you are about to begin applying the practices of character and virtue education to your own life. As you do so, you need to make a conscious choice. Do you intentionally *want to do* something to shape your character according to virtue as part of your walk of Christian discipleship?

This is the important emphasis of this week.

Wrestle with the Questions

Take a few minutes to honestly wrestle with the following four questions:

1. Do you *want* to be more virtuous? Being a virtuous person starts with *desiring* personal transformation. This requires an attitude of humility, where you recognize that you are not what you would like to be and that you want to change. Without this desire you will never grow in virtue. Have you thought this through? Do you really want to move away from vice and be more virtuous?

2. Do you have the right *motivation*? It is not sufficient to simply desire virtue, you must also desire it for the right reasons. Don't choose virtue just because it seems like a useful thing to do. And don't choose virtue because you are burdened by guilt. Neither of these motivations will hold out on the long term. Instead, choose to be virtuous because you want to flourish as a human being and because you see this as a high expression of love toward God, neighbour and yourself.

3. Are you willing to be *accountable*? Virtue education is not something that is easily done alone. There is a long and difficult road ahead of you, and you will find great benefit in making a *covenant in a community* to help you in this journey. If you are working with a group, you already have this advantage. If you are going through this workbook alone, you will be shown in the coming weeks how to identify character friends with whom you can be vulnerable and accountable. Is this something you are willing to do?

4. Are you available to bear the *pain of change*? As is the case with most change in our lives, educating your character in virtue will involve some pain. This might be physical pain (for example, from physical exercise), relational pain, intellectual pain or the pain that comes with disciplining yourself to do things that you do not feel like doing. Are you willing to pay the price of virtue?

These are all very important questions. If this discipleship project is to have any real influence on your life, you need to consider them carefully before God. In the Act section below, you will be given an opportunity to make a written commitment.

The Virtue of Constancy

Before your write your commitment, there is a fundamental virtue that you need to wrestle with. This is the virtue of *constancy*.

Constancy is another one of those beautiful old words that has fallen into disuse. And as we remove constancy from our vocabulary, we risk losing its focus on the need for firmness and determination in searching for what is good, in resisting temptation, in overcoming sloth, in demonstrating strength of resolve, in bending our will to reasoned choices and in overcoming the obstacles of moral life.

Constancy comes together with *loyalty*, both in relationships and in causes, and with *perseverance*, in facing trials, difficulties and persecutions. Constancy is the long walk in the same direction. It is the marathon of life rather than a set of short sprints. Constancy and perseverance may be to the point of death as has been the case for many Christian martyrs. Constancy creates the kind of stability that allows you to complete your life's projects.

Many contemporary societies have replaced the virtue constancy with the pursuit of freedom, and this has led to a proliferation of the vices of *fickleness*, where commitments are made and easily unmade, of *whimsicalness*, where the wind of emotion and circumstance governs choices, of *superficiality* and its thin veneer of appearances that have no underlying foundations, and of *irresponsibility*, where we refuse to be tied down to situations that bind us in any way.

When it comes to educating your character for virtue, constancy is a foundational virtue. Through constancy, virtue education will either succeed or fail. As you will soon learn, virtue education involves developing new habits of character, and these take time to consolidate. This workbook assumes several months of intensive practice in order to begin to form character shaping habits. But these will only bear fruit if you are constant over time.

So here is a final question: will you be *constant*? Are you ready to persevere over a long time? In choosing this project of virtue education, do you commit to finish it even if you get tired, distracted, bored or not see immediate results?

Verify

You are about to put your commitment in writing, but first verify your understanding of the terms of the commitment.[16]

(a) Wanting to be more virtuous involves your _____ .

(b) Choosing virtue as an expression of love toward God, neighbour and yourself has to do with right _____ .

(c) You will need character friends with whom to be _____

  and _____ .

(d) Changing your character will involve some _____ .

(e) Virtue education will either succeed or fail because of _____ .

Act: Writing Your Commitment and Creating a Reminder

Are you ready to commit? Use the following prompts to prayerfully express your commitment in writing.

I really want to be more virtuous. In particular, here are some of the virtues/vices that I know I need to work on . . .

My motivation to be more virtuous is . . .

Here are the names of those to whom I would like to be accountable about my character growth . . .

Change will be difficult, but I think that . . .

Concerning constancy, here is my aim . . .

To help yourself remain constant in your commitment, create a visual reminder. This can be whatever you want, so be creative. Here are some ideas:

- Create a small card to put on your desk with a slogan or motto related to virtue education. You might use online word clouds or meme generators to do this.
- Create a small piece of art relative to character, virtue and education (this will depend on how artistic you are, but it could be a painting, graphic design, sculpture or even a song if you are a musician).
- Create a screensaver with an image that reminds you of virtue.
- Make a small bookmark to use as you read more about virtue.
- Generate a wish list of books and movies on virtue. Then set up a reminder to read/watch something at regular intervals.
- Set up a weekly notification in your smartphone with a question, a reminder or a word of encouragement to yourself to remain constant in your commitment to virtue education.
- Make yourself a little bracelet with knots in it – as a reminder of reminders.
- Get yourself something to wear, like a T-Shirt printed with a slogan, or a cap with "virtue" written on it.
- Make a small monument and put it somewhere where you will see it often. This could be, for example, a small pile of rocks in a V shape, to remind you of the word virtue.

These visual reminders should not be underestimated or considered childish. The world is full of meaningful monuments that shape us and of visual advertisements that condition our choices. So here is your chance to be intentional in conditioning yourself through your own visual reminder of virtue.

† Bible Study: Being Stiff-Necked

Read: Exodus 32:9

To build on this week's lesson that has focused on making a commitment to your character and virtue education journey, here is a short Bible study that will help prepare you for the coming weeks.

The book of Exodus presents us with an extensive case study of growth and decline in the character of the people of Israel. Their story is sadly marked by failure and lack of constancy. In Exodus 32:9 God makes an evaluation of the character of his people and concludes that they have one main vice: they are "stiff-necked" (see also 33:3 and 34:9).

What does this mean, and how might it relate to your own character?

The term "stiff-necked" (in Hebrew: *qasheh*) means "resistant to pressure." In our text, it is applied to the people of Israel who were resistant to the positive pressures that God was putting on their lives to model faithful and obedient character. In Exodus these positive pressures take the form of miracles, of divine punishment, of judgement on Pharaoh, of crossing the Red Sea, and so forth. All of these episodes were positive pressures that were meant to shape their character. And all were potentially conducive to helping them grow in faith and obedience.

But that did not happen. They were stiff-necked and resistant to what God was doing to shape them. Their story is marked by resistance to virtue, resulting in faithlessness, disobedience and eventually ruin.

Take some time now to find answers to the following questions from other texts in Exodus:

1. What were the factors that negatively influenced the character of Israel and kept them from developing the virtues of faith and obedience? Find at least two or three factors from reading these stories: 13:17, 14:12, 15:24, 16:2–3, 17:3, 32:8.

2. Were the Israelites always stiff-necked? Read: 19:8, 14:31, 24:3, 7. What do these episodes say about inconstancy and how it relates to being stiff-necked?

3. In the overall story of Exodus, how was God's grace at work as he dealt with the character flaws of the people of Israel?

Now respond. Think of your own life. What positive pressures has God put on your life to change your character and nourish virtue? How and why have you resisted them? What should your appropriate response have been? How might the opportunity offered by working through this workbook on character and virtue education represent a chance for you to not be "stiff-necked"?

Write your answers to these questions in the box below.

A Prayer

Lord, I recognize in myself the tendency to be stiff-necked and not change. Give me the grace of being responsive to your call to virtue and of being constant in my commitment to it.

> This week you have made a commitment to a journey of character and virtue education. Next week you will begin this journey with a self-assessment test.

Date completed: _____

Week 6

Take the Virtue Test

Self-assess your character in light of the virtues

This week you will self-assess your character through a tool called the Virtue Test. This is an important practical step in your virtue education experience. Before you take the test, however, it is helpful to understand what it is and what to expect from it.

Self-Assessment

Let's start by talking briefly about self-assessment.

Self-assessment is a practice that helps you see yourself honestly, recognizing your flaws and your achievements. Self-assessment itself requires the cultivation of two main virtues: *humility* and *prudence*.

Humility is essential for healthy self-assessment because it removes a spirit of self-justification, self-defence and false modesty and allows you to gain a clear vision of your strengths and weaknesses. Self-assessment will rarely work in the presence of pride.

Prudence is essential for healthy self-assessment because it gives you the ability to reflect on the practices of virtue in your everyday life. You will learn more about prudence in Week 23, but for now understand it as the practical wisdom that allows you to see yourself as you really are and helps you discern which virtues are necessary as you meet life's unpredictable circumstances.

How the Virtue Test Works

The online Virtue Test you are about to take is an exercise in self-assessment. So how does it work? It is quite simple, and if you have ever taken a personality test, you will find that it is similar.

The online test has 100 brief statements, each of which is connected to a specific virtue. You will respond to each statement, ranking how it describes you: never, rarely, occasionally, frequently or always. In tests like this one, responders usually gravitate toward the more moderate answers "in the middle" and stay away from the "never" and "always" answers. If in doubt, choose a more extreme answer as this will make your results clearer. The purpose is not necessarily to score well, but to produce a score that is useful in your self-assessment.

At the end of the test you will see your score in thirteen different virtues. Higher scores will indicate strengths of virtue in your character. Lower scores will indicate virtues that you might need to work on.

Ready? Complete the brief quiz opposite to ensure your understanding and then proceed to take the test.

✅ Verify

Verify your understanding of assessment and of what the Virtue Test is.[17]

(a) What are the two virtues that you need to perform healthy self-assessment?

_____ and _____

(b) The Virtue Test helps you assess your character against thirteen common virtues.

☐ True
☐ False

(c) The Virtue Test is only available online.

☐ True
☐ False

(d) Which choice gives clearer results: "moderate" answers or more "extreme" ones?

_____

(e) You will receive a numerical score of your results.

☐ True
☐ False

👥 Act: Take the Virtue Test

Take the online Virtue Test in one sitting (the test is only available online and it is not possible to save it and resume). Allow about twenty minutes to answer all 100 questions.

Provide your email to receive a copy of your results. The test is anonymous.

Scan this QR code to access the Virtue Test.[18] You will need a valid internet connection.

Take the test now.

Once you have completed the test you will see your scores on a scale of 0–100 (you will also receive a copy of numerical results by email). Please record these scores here:

Your score in virtue of PRUDENCE is _____

Your score in virtue of TEMPERANCE is _____

Your score in virtue of COURAGE is _____

Your score in virtue of JUSTICE is _____

Your score in virtue of HUMILITY is _____

Your score in virtue of CONSTANCY is _____

Your score in virtue of TRUTHFULNESS is _____

Your score in virtue of COMPASSION is _____

Your score in virtue of PRUDENCE is _____

Your score in virtue of FAITH is _____

Your score in virtue of HOPE is _____

Write the three virtues in which you have scored lowest:

_____, _____, _____

That is enough for this week. Next week you will be helped to interpret your results and you will select one virtue in particular on which to work.

📖 Bible Study: Look in the Mirror

Read: James 1:22–25

This week you have thought about self-assessment, and you have completed the Virtue Test to assess your own character. The metaphor that we find in James 1 of looking at yourself in a mirror is a wonderful summary of some of the main features of self-assessment. Notice the following.

First, self-assessment **begins with instruction**. James claims that "hearing the word" is the first step in the direction of changed behaviour. In this workbook, you are receiving instruction about character and about your responsibility as a disciple to intentionally pursue virtue. You have also "heard the word" about what virtues are, and this has laid the ground for your self-assessment.

Second, self-assessment **involves an intense activity of looking** at our "natural" faces. James indicates that we are to concentrate on seeing who we really are. We do not usually do this. Especially concerning our moral self. But this is what you have just done through the Virtue Test.

Third, self-assessment must **lead to action**. James reminds us that looking at ourselves is not an end in itself. We should be "doing the word." This is potentially the weakest spot in self-assessment. Mere evaluation without self-improvement is, in the words of James, self-deceit. That is why the main emphasis of this workbook as you move ahead will be on practice.

Finally, self-assessment, when properly done, **leads to flourishing**. James claims that as we hear, look and do we will be "blessed." Hopefully, as you grow in character and virtue you will experience a growing sense of wellbeing and deep happiness.

Now respond: Examine your walk of discipleship against the four features outlined by James. You may want to use the following prompts: Which of the four features is the weakest in your life? How do you respond to criticism and to negative assessment? Did you tend to overestimate your scores in the Virtue Test? Do you fall into the pitfall of evaluation without self-improvement? How good are you at celebrating your own victories?

 A Prayer

Lord grant that I may hear your word. Then open my eyes to see myself as I truly am. Then give the strength and constancy to do that which will shape what I am. And as I find happiness, remind me to return to you in gratefulness.

> This week you have taken the Virtue Test as a first step towards intentional work on your character. Next week you will be led to understand your results and to focus on one virtue with which to begin.

Date completed: _____

Week 7

Interpreting the Virtue Test

Understand the results of your Virtue Test

L ast week you completed the Virtue Test and noted the scores for each virtue. This week you will interpret the results of this test.

Generally speaking, the scores can be understood as follows:

- A score between 75–100 indicates that a virtue is well established in your character. Well done.
- A score between 45–75 indicates that there is room to grow in your character. This may be where you want to concentrate.
- A score between 0–45 indicates a possible problem related to the absence of a virtue. You should carefully prioritize these lower scores as you make plans for growth.

The plan for character and virtue education in this workbook is based on working on one virtue at a time, and you will soon be selecting one virtue on which to work. Before you make this choice, however, take some time to sharpen your results.

Virtue Test Disclaimer

Self-assessment tests based on numerical algorithms like the Virtue Test are fallible and may not be very accurate. You should therefore not blindly trust the numerical score of your test.

It would be a mistake, for example, to simply take the lowest score of your test and choose to work on that virtue, as you may have scored yourself more harshly or more generously on one virtue compared to others. Also, while there are good reasons to work on your "weaker" virtues, there is no need to think that you should necessarily work on your "weakest" virtue.

Treat the scores of your test as indicative and not as final. Although they give you some important leads, if you want to obtain sharper results take some time to reflect further along the lines suggested below.

One important way of sharpening your reflection on the virtues is to understand the ways in which virtues can fall into vice. Each virtue, in fact, can go wrong in different directions and fall into different vices.

For most virtues, in fact, there is more than one possible vice. The virtue of *justice*, for example, can go wrong through the vice of *indifference*, but it can also fall short and produce the vices of *dishonesty* or *unfairness*. Likewise, the virtue of *generosity* can fall into the vice of *greed*, but it can arguably also go too far and fall into the vice of *irresponsibility*. And so on.

Aristotle suggests that virtues fail either by excess or defect and that virtue is always found in a harmonic "middle" (*in medio stat virtus*). So, for example, if the results of your Virtue Test indicated a low score in the virtue of *courage* this could mean two things. It might indicate that you are negatively conditioned by fear and that you need to correct the vice of *cowardice*. But it may also mean that you have gone too far in the other direction, with an excessive disdain of fear, and that would mean working on the vice of *recklessness*. This kind of reflection is very important, as there is the danger of working on the right virtue, but in the wrong direction. And that would only make your vice worse!

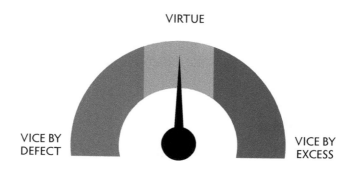

In Week 2 you saw the vices-by-excess and vices-by-defect in the Virtue Wheel (see also below). The table below summarizes how the thirteen virtues in the Virtue Test might fall into vice either by excess or by defect.

Vice-by-defect	Virtue	Vice-by-excess
Cowardice	**Courage**	Recklessness
Stupidity	**Prudence**	Paranoia
Extreme submission	**Justice**	Violence
Self-indulgence	**Temperance**	Extreme self-denial
Pride	**Humility**	Self-annulment
Fickleness	**Constancy**	Obstinacy
Dishonesty/lying	**Truthfulness**	Indiscretion
Indifference	**Compassion**	Indiscrimination
Cynicism	**Faith**	Naivety
Undue negativism	**Hope**	Undue optimism
No love for others	**Love**	No love for self
Laziness	**Diligence**	Obsession with duty
Ignorance	**Knowledge**	Intellectual pride

Use this table to sharpen your focus, taking some time to ponder it now. Look at the lower scores in your test results again and put an "X" next to the vices that you gravitate towards (either in the left- or right-hand column). This should be an indication of whether you scored lower in the virtue because of excess or because of defect, and it will show you with greater precision where you need to work in your character.

Understanding of the Virtues

Now is a good time to read a little more about individual virtues. Leaving aside your test results for a moment, look at the Virtue Wheel again. Which of these do you feel you should be working on?

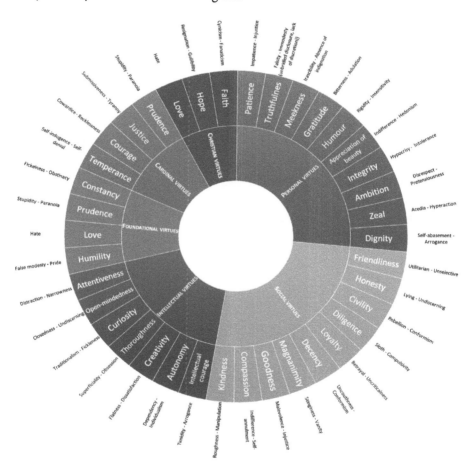

If you want to read a little bit more of any of the virtues that were analysed through the Virtue Test, use the QR code below to consult a set of brief definitions.

(Virtues Unpacked)[19]

Spend about 15 minutes browsing through these definitions, making sure you include the virtues that you have scored lowest on.

As you read more about each virtue, ask yourself the questions: Is this describing me? Do I feel that this is an area of weakness in my character that I need to work on? Is this virtue the one that I would like to have more of in this stage of my life? Which vices do I recognize in my character that are detracting from this virtue?

Use the box below to take some notes as you look at these virtues.

✅ Verify

Verify your understanding of the virtues. Match each statement (a-m) with the corresponding virtue (1–13):[20]

1) Compassion   _____

2) Constancy   _____

3) Courage   _____

4) Diligence   _____

5) Faith   _____

6) Hope   _____

7) Humility   _____

8) Justice   _____

9) Knowledge   _____

10) Love   _____

(a) Its vice-by-defect is cynicism. Its vice-by-excess is ingenuity.

(b) It comes together with decency as living in conformity to right standards of purity, cleanliness and dignity.

(c) Without this virtue you will never work on other virtues in your character.

(d) Opposing vices can be simple-mindedness, disregard for beauty, distraction and intellectual pride.

(e) The long walk in the same direction.

(f) It contains and motivates all the other virtues.

(g) The virtue that helps you to deploy the right virtue at the appropriate time.

(h) Governing yourself through reason, being content with your state and being able to tame your impulses and appetites.

(i) An active disposition towards sharing and supporting those who are facing adverse circumstances.

(j) It comes with the virtues of responsibility, loyalty and honesty.

11) Prudence _____   (k) The actioned desire that what is due should be given in order to favour the ideal interaction between individuals in a community.

12) Temperance _____   (l) It is related to the virtue of patience in calling for appropriate and temporary resignation regarding the evils of the world.

13) Truthfulness _____   (m) Facing fearful situations that are larger than you are, and you nevertheless bend your will to do your duty.

Act: Choose One Virtue to Work On

Now that you have completed your self-assessment and interpreted the results of the Virtue Test, it is time to choose one virtue on which you will begin to work.

Virtue education, in fact, works best when you focus on one virtue at a time. In the future, you can repeat the growth plan and work on other virtues. But for now, just focus on one virtue.

As a result of this week, you should have identified one virtue (and perhaps a corresponding specific vice) to work on. Write the name of this virtue in the box below. This will be your main focus in the coming months.

You may wish to go back to the visual reminder that you created two weeks ago and now add this specific virtue.

Incidentally, don't be too concerned about getting all this exactly right. The most important thing is that you have decided to consciously work on your character, and there is no danger of working on "the wrong virtue." You have your entire lifetime to work on the virtues. So any work, on any virtue, is always right.

⊞ Bible Study: You Are the Man!

Read: 2 Samuel 12:1–13

As you progress through this growth plan, this week you have made an important choice to focus on a particular virtue. As Christians, we believe that God has a part in our choices and that he is interested in speaking to us about our character. The Bible study this week speaks to this.

2 Samuel tells the story about Nathan confronting David's sin with Bathsheba. Notice several things from the story:

God wants to speak to you about your character. We read, in fact, that "God sent Nathan to David" (12:1). God took the initiative with David, and he takes initiatives with you when it comes to improving your character.

God speaks clearly. You may fear that you have not "heard the voice of God." This story shows us that God does all that is possible to make himself heard. Do not worry, he wants to speak to you even more than you want to hear. In this case, God gets David's attention by rousing strong emotions in him through the story of the rich and poor men and their lambs (12:1–6).

God uses people in your life to make his voice even clearer. David is dull in his understanding, and even after listening to the story, he still does not understand that it is about him. It takes Nathan's explicit words "You are the man!" (12:7), before he finally hears the true message. Might it be the same with you? If you are oblivious to the voice of God, he might use human messengers to make the message even clearer. Perhaps you should talk to someone who knows you well about your choice of a virtue.

There is a "then" moment. This little word "then" (12:13) marks a huge moment in David's life. He was not performing a correct assessment of his life and God spoke to him. *Then* he heard. And this is the hope for you. As you actively ask which virtue to work on in your life, you will hear the voice of God.

Perhaps this happened as you took the virtue test, or while you were reading more about the virtues and their vices, or maybe you were struck by a particular vice that did not appear specifically in your results. Maybe you felt a tug toward a virtue on which you need to work. Listen carefully to these signs for they could be the voice of God.

And now for a final point.

Notice that this text describes the lack of virtue as sin. Although this workbook normally uses the positive terminology of the virtues to encourage growth, it can also be helpful to use the negative terminology of the vices.

In David's case there were several virtues missing, including *temperance* and *justice*, but there were also multiple vices, including *lust* and *deceit*. Notice that in his "then" moment, David does not exclaim "I think I need to work on some virtues in my character." Instead he says: "I have sinned."

Now respond: Repentance is an ongoing practice of discipleship. Use the space below to confess the vices/sins which you are determined to change.

A Prayer

Lord speak to me as I search my heart desiring virtue. Show me vices where you would have me change. If necessary, send a Nathan to me. I repent of sin in my character which is habitual and pray that you will grant me the opportunity to change.

> This week you have been helped to understand the results of your Virtue Test and to choose one virtue in particular. Next week you will learn about the tools that can help you to begin growing this virtue in your life.

Date completed: _____

Week 8

A Plan for Practice

Develop an intentional plan to grow in virtue

L ast week you identified a virtue on which you would like to work. This week you will begin to develop an intensive practice plan to develop this virtue. This plan will take about 15 weeks to complete.

So you are now beginning the longest and the hardest part. Are you ready?

A Multi-Faceted Tool Set

There are several tools that can work together to educate your character for virtue. In this workbook, three tools have been selected. They are habituation, character friendship and virtue literacy. You will learn more about each in greater detail in the weeks to come, but here is an initial description.

1) **Habituation**. Although it may seem paradoxical, doing is a prelude to becoming. That means that you can shape who you are by creating habits in what you do. Habituation is an *intentional* repetition of virtuous actions to create habits of character.

2) **Character friendship**. Character is not shaped in a vacuum but in a community, and in particular through friendships marked by the shared commitment to virtue. Character friendship is an *intentional* pursuit of a personal relationship of accountability.

3) **Virtue literacy**. Virtue literacy is an *intentional* engagement with concepts and stories of virtue that model your mind, generate desires of emulation. These have a deep and long-lasting effect on your character.

The Importance of Intention

You may have noticed that the word *intention* has been highlighted in all three tools. None of these tools, in fact, is automatic and they are effective only as you continually and deliberately choose to use them. As you have already seen in previous weeks, the key in fulfilling your intentions is constancy.

What does the Bible teach about intention? In 1 Corinthians 9 Paul reminds us that running a race requires strict training and intentional strategy. This workbook offers you some intentional strategies and a training plan, but it has no magic formula for success. It is up to you to maintain the firmness of your training and maintain your actions in line with your intentions.

Remember, character and virtue are shaped slowly over time, constancy is the key, and discipleship is a long walk in the same direction.

Progressively Using These Tools

Good planning is an important part in running our race well. So what plan will you follow in using the tools of habituation, character friendship and virtue literacy?

In this workbook these three tools will be introduced incrementally. This means that, rather than beginning to use all three tools at once, you will begin using them one at a time and then gradually build up to using all three. Over the next few weeks you will start with habituation, then you will add character friendship, and then you will add virtue literacy. As you add each new tool, you will continue practicing the previous tools, benefitting from an incremental effect (first one tool, then two and finally all three together).

Here is the outline of this plan:

Week 9	Week 11	Week 13		Week 23

HABITUATION

CHARACTER FRIENDSHIP

VIRTUE LITERACY

In summary:

- In Week 9 and 10 you will be led to develop a habituation plan. You will then practice it for thirteen weeks.
- In Week 11 you will add the element of character friendship. You then practice this for twelve weeks (in addition to practicing your habituation plan).
- In Week 13 you will add the third element of virtue literacy as you engage a different virtue every week for nine weeks (in addition to practicing your habituation plan and your character friendship contract).

Do not worry if you have not fully grasped the logistics and the planning of what is ahead. Each week you will receive explanations and instructions on what to do.

Verify

Verify your understanding of the tools you will be using in character and virtue education.[21]

(a) Character and virtue education is an automatic process.

    ❏ True ❏ False

(b) The repetition of virtuous actions that creates habits of character is called

_____.

(c) The pursuit of a personal relationship of accountability for your character is called

_____.

(d) Your mind can be modelled and your desires for emulation stimulated through

_____.

(e) The most important thing in the three tools we will be using for character education is

_____.

(f) You will be introduced to all three tools for character and virtue education at the same time.

    ❏ True ❏ False

Act: Put the Plan in Your Calendar

It is important that what you will be doing in the coming weeks finds its way into your personal calendar. If it helps, take some time to browse ahead through the contents of the next thirteen weeks in this workbook.

Use the space below to:

- Note the dates of when you will be engaging with habituation.
- Note the dates of when you will be engaging with character friendship and of when you should plan specific meetings with your character friend.
- Note the dates of when virtue literacy will be developed.

You are strongly encouraged to insert these dates into a calendar now (either physical or digital). If you use a smart phone app, this can be very useful to set up reminders.

If you are working with a group, you will be looking at these dates during this week's meeting.

Bible Study: Virtue and the Spirit

Read: Galatians 5 and 6

This week you've thought about intention and of the importance of you taking responsibility for your character growth. But what does the Bible say about intention?

The Bible study this week develops a very important question that was mentioned a few weeks ago. Is becoming more virtuous something that *God* does in you, or is it something that *you* achieve through your intentions?

You have already seen how the "fruit of the Spirit" in Galatians relates to the virtues. This week you will return to this text to see what it teaches about human agency and divine intervention.

Begin by reading the entire chapter of Galatians 5 with two questions in mind: "What is God doing?" and "What are we asked to do?" As you read, complete the following tables and match the given statements with the corresponding verses.

What God does	Verse
The Spirit shapes our desires	_____
The Spirit leads us	_____
The Spirit produces fruit in us	_____

What we do	Verse
We are called to not indulge in the flesh	_____
It is our responsibility to walk by the Spirit	_____
We are not to gratify the desires of the flesh	_____

As you can see, on the one hand, it is the responsibility of the follower of Christ to "not indulge," to "walk by the Spirit," and to govern the "conflict" between competing desires. On the other hand, God works in us as the work of the Spirit "leads us," "shapes our desires," and gives us the ability to bear virtuous fruit.

The teaching of this passage is that there is an interplay between you and the Spirit. In this interplay the desires of the Spirit influence your own desires in such a way that the desires of the flesh, which once came naturally to you, are replaced by a Spirit-driven desire for virtue. Through these new, Spirit-infused desires, the fruit of the Spirit comes "naturally." The Spirit comes alongside your efforts to supernaturally shape your desires, and enable you to enjoy virtue and be virtuous.

So, looking at the "you" side of the equation, what should your efforts to be virtuous look like? Read Galatians 6 and note the description of ten elements that show us in practice what we need to do as we live a life led by the Spirit.

Match the following statements with the verses in Galatians 6:

1) We need to have clear ideas on sin/vice   _____

2) We need to practice gentle restoration   _____

3) We need to watch out for temptation   _____

4) We need to be in community, carrying each other's burdens   _____

5) We need to remain humble   _____

6) We need to test our actions through self-assessment   _____

7) We can find legitimate pride in the achievement of good character   _____

8) We should stay away from comparisons   _____

9) We must feel responsible for ourselves   _____

10) We should be grateful for good instructors   _____

Now respond: How can you put the ten elements from Galatians 6 into practice as you work your way through this workbook? Choose four of the elements in the list above and rewrite them in your own words, applying them to your character growth intentions.

A Prayer

My commitment Lord is to not indulge in vice, to be on the watch for vice in my life, to walk by the Spirit in a commitment to virtue and to govern the conflicts between my competing desires. As I do so, I ask that your Spirit lead me, shape my desires and give me the ability to bear virtuous fruit.

This week you have been introduced to the tools that will help you grow in character and virtue. Next week you will begin using them.

Date completed: _____

Week 9

What Is Habituation

Understand the habituation process

You are now about one third of your way through this workbook. So far you have gained some foundational knowledge about virtue education, you have self-assessed your character and you have identified one virtue on which you want to work.

Now, it is time to begin an intensive practice phase, and begin using the tool of habituation. So let's start with the basics, what exactly is habituation?

Education through Habituation

There are many ways in which humans can be educated, and habituation is one of these.

Habituation is easily understood by thinking about how we get to be good at doing anything. Think, for example, about playing the piano. How do you get good at it? Those who play well know that the real secret is found in countless hours of repetition. Piano students repeat scales so many times that finding the right notes on the keyboard becomes a built-in habit. As they repeat their scales, they are being "habituated into a practice" until ability, harmony, rhythm and the ability to improvise become natural.

Habits and repetition have a powerful ability to shape us for good. But they also have the power of shaping us negatively. Most examples of addiction are, for example, related to developing wrong habits. And this applies to virtue and vice. Virtue is cultivated by habituating virtuous actions. Vice is cultivated by habituating viceful actions.

Aristotle is one of many who have written about habituation. He claims that you are educated in virtue in the same way as you are educated in a technical ability, which is by constant repetition and habit building. In practice, you initially choose to repeat virtuous actions as an act of your will. But as you repeat virtuous actions, they become habits, and then these habits become a "second nature" and shape your soul. The Christian theologian Thomas Aquinas summarized this well with the claim that "human virtues are habits."

So, for example, by practising actions of justice, we become more *just*. As we face our fears, we become more *courageous*. As we give, we become more *generous*, and as we abstain from excesses, we become more *temperate*.

The key, initially, is conscious choice and wilful repetition. The statement Aristotle made that "one swallow does not make spring" suggests that it is not sufficient for one swallow to fly over our heads to proclaim that spring has arrived. It is only when many swallows fly constantly in the air that we can be really sure that the season has changed. And so it is with virtue. Our character is not changed by doing one or two virtuous actions, but by long and continued repetition.

The Roman saying *Gutta cava lapidem* (a drip of water shapes the rock), reminds us that through slow, continual repetition, the smallest drop of water will eventually wear through the hardest rock. Slow persistency goes against contemporary capitalist culture that demands speed, high impact and efficiency. Sadly, we sometimes see these same attitudes in Christian discipleship as we expect easy recipes to accomplish everything quickly and well. We need to unlearn these attitudes and reclaim practices like habituation that are based on slowness, constancy and deep change.

Here are five points that can help you remember what habituation is:

1) Even if you are not yet virtuous you can perform virtuous actions.

2) You can shape what you are through the habits of what you do.

3) As you repeat virtuous actions, habits of virtue are formed.

4) As you form virtue habits, your character is gradually shaped to be "naturally" virtuous.

5) Habituation has to do initially with the exercise of the will but eventually produces spontaneous action.

Habituation does not guarantee character growth for everyone, but if you are rightly motivated and determined it is a powerful tool of change.

Verify

Briefly verify your understanding of habituation.[22]

(a) Habituation is one of the three tools that will be used in your plan for practice. ☐ True ☐ False

(b) What has deep power in shaping who we are (for good or for bad)?

_____

(c) Aristotle said that virtues are made perfect by _____.

(d) Aquinas said that "human virtues are _____."

(e) Even if you are not virtuous, you can perform virtuous actions and thereby become virtuous. ☐ True ☐ False

(f) Habituation has to do with the exercise of the _____.

Act: Identify Activities, Opportunities and Habits

To help you think about how habituation might relate to the virtue you identified in Week 7, you will now list a couple of actions that are related to the virtue you want to develop. Think of opportunities to practice them and then name the habit that these actions might develop.

To help you understand the exercise, here are a couple of examples.

Do you remember the story of Beatrice in Week 1? She had chosen to develop the virtue of justice. Here is what this exercise might have looked like for her:

Beatrice's chosen virtue	Activity/action (what she wanted to do)	Opportunity (when she wanted to do this)	The habit she wanted to develop
Justice	Obey traffic rules	Every time she drove her car	Beatrice wanted to develop the habit of respecting rules and the rights of others

Here is a second example that might relate to you. Imagine that the virtue you want to develop is gratitude. Here is what the exercise might look like:

My chosen virtue	Activity/action (what I want to do)	Opportunity (when I want to do this)	The habit I want to develop
Gratitude	Write a thank you message to a friend or relative	Every Sunday morning for the entire summer	I want to develop the habit of saying thank you

Now it is your turn. Write your chosen virtue in column 1. Then try to think of at least two actions and opportunities that might contribute to building a new virtuous habit.

My chosen virtue	Activity/action 1 (what I want to do)	Opportunity 1 (when I want to do this)	The habit I want to develop
	Activity/action 2 (what I want to do)	Opportunity 2 (when I want to do this)	

This may not have been easy. But do not worry. Next week you will build on these initial thoughts and receive instructions on how to write a well-articulated habituation plan.

☐ Bible Study: The Ten Words as Virtue Habituation

Read: Exodus 20:1–17

This week's Bible study builds on what you have learned about habituation by offering some reflections on the Ten Commandments. You have probably never thought of the Ten Commandments in terms of virtue habituation, so this might be something new.

The word "commandments" is not always helpful, as it can make us think of orders, rules and laws that are given and that need to be externally obeyed. But this is not the full picture.

Exodus 20 specifies that God "spoke" a set of words. The Greek translation of the Old Testament (the Septuagint), in fact, uses the term *dekalogos* which literally means "ten words." So how do these words have a shaping effect as tools of virtue?

As a preliminary thought, notice that the Ten Words include the tools that you saw last week for character education.

- There is character friendship. These Ten Words are not given to individuals, but to a community. And that community was bound together in a walk of obedience to God.
- There is virtue literacy. These Ten Words are not just given. They were explained in greater depth in Exodus, they were repeated again in Deuteronomy, and they were brought to life by the stories of the people of Israel as they obeyed or disobeyed them.

But most of all, in the Ten Words we see habituation. These Ten Words were meant to enter into the daily routine of the people of Israel. To help the formation of habits around these words, God tells Israel to continually read and dwell on them, to establish yearly festivals and regular sacrifices, to continually instruct their children and to create visual reminders.

In Deuteronomy 6 we have explicit instructions concerning the habituation of these words:

> These commandments that I give you today are to be on your hearts. Impress them on your children. Talk about them when you sit at home and when you walk along the road, when you lie down and when you get up. Tie them as symbols on your hands and bind them on your foreheads. Write them on the doorframes of your houses and on your gates. (6:6–9)

So we have much more than a list of rules. God sets up a genuine three step habit-building programme to shape the character of his people that begins with commandments around actions, is reinforced by a context of repetition to create habits, and culminates in virtuous character.

The table below illustrates these three steps for the first two commandments:

Commandment to action	The habit that is created	The virtue that becomes part of character
Have no other gods	Worship is offered regularly and exclusively to Jehovah	Faithfulness
Do not use the name of God in vain	Telling the truth without having to swear by God	Honesty

Now respond: Now try to complete the table for the other eight commandments in Deuteronomy 20:1–17.

Commandment to action	The habit that is created	The virtue that becomes part of character
Do not make graven images		
Remember the Sabbath		
Honour your father and mother		
Do not kill		
Do not commit adultery		
Do not steal		
Do not bear false witness		
Do not covet		

A Prayer

To God who has spoken these Ten Words I wish to express my gratitude. Thank you for these guidelines that are here to shape us into your people and make us flourishing human beings. May they become habits in my life, together with the people with whom I am called to walk. And may they shape my character in virtue.

> This week you have gained some understanding of the
> practice of habituation. Next week you will craft a specific
> habituation plan to grow in your chosen virtue.

Date completed: _____

Week 10

Planning for Virtue

Make a habituation plan for the coming months

N ow is the time to become very practical and define a habituation plan for the coming months. By the end of this week, you should have a written plan and next week you will begin putting it into practice.

Start Small but Specific

Some of the things that you have read about so far in this workbook may have sounded pretty grandiose. And, to some extent, education of virtue is grandiose. But when it comes to practice, virtue education amounts to working on the small things in your life. The plan that you are going to develop for the coming months is not likely to completely fix all of your character flaws nor will it make you perfectly virtuous. But it will help you achieve some significant goals.

What then, makes a good habituation plan? To keep things simple, try using the familiar SMART matrix. Your habituation plan needs to be specific (S), measurable (M), achievable (A), relevant (R) and time bound (T). Here are examples of good and bad plans.

- Example of a really bad plan: *I will improve the virtue of compassion by helping those that are needy.* This plan is relevant, but it is not specific, measurable, achievable or time bound.
- Example of a bad plan: *I will improve the virtue of compassion by helping the sick people in my city.* This is a little more specific, but still not measurable, achievable or time bound.

- Example of a good plan: *I will improve the virtue of compassion by doing volunteer work with the children in the cancer ward of my local hospital.* This is specific and achievable, but it can still improve in terms of being measurable and time bound.
- Example of a really good plan: *I will improve the virtue of compassion by doing volunteer work in the cancer ward of my local hospital with at least two children every Saturday morning for the next five months.* This is SMART.

Some Examples

Here now are some real-life examples of habituation plans (names have been changed):

Cherian: My chosen virtue is *temperance* with particular relation to the time I spend on social media. It has previously been the case that large portions of my time were spent on my phone or laptop, scrolling through social media, rather than doing something productive. In order to balance this out, I will give myself a daily limit of fifteen minutes on social media. I will do this by setting up a screen time alarm which will notify me once my daily time has been reached.

Linda: My chosen virtues are *courage* and *generosity*, as I recognize the need to reach out to new people and be generous in my time with them. I plan to talk to one new student in my university every week, to initiate a conversation with them, getting to know them and even offering my time to know or help them with anything if needed. This habituation will take me out of my comfort zone of only speaking with or clinging to the same people I know and feel comfortable with.

Golan: My chosen virtue is *compassion* in helping others. For five months I will offer to cook at least once a week for my family and whenever there is washing up to do, I will volunteer rather than waiting for someone else to do it. This is a realistic target for me. In order to improve my sympathy towards others I will also pray for at least one person in need every night. This is a feasible achievement as all I need to do is to remember to pray for others.

Dmitry: My chosen virtue is *generosity*. I was struck during the Virtue Test that this is a lack of love. I have seen that I lack generosity both towards others and towards myself, as I rarely allow myself any "extra" good things. My plan is hence twofold. In order to be more generous to others, I will ensure that I regularly attend church and serve where I have said I would, even when it is not convenient for me. This will instil in me the importance of sharing generously with my time. Second, in order to be more generous toward myself, when I go to the grocery shop, I will make sure that I buy at least one or two items which are more of a luxury or some kind of treat. Both these activities will take place over a period of six months, and I will keep a note of my progress in my journal.

Promise: My chosen virtue is *hope* as I recognize the potential vice of cynicism in me. To do this, each time I make a negative comment about a situation, I want to force myself to make a positive comment as well. I often find myself making a negative comment about a person, but I want to make a positive comment too. At the end of each day, I will make a note in my phone calendar of one time that I have consciously made a positive comment following a negative one.

As you can see, these plans are very different from each other, but they are all simple and specific.

Remember, Remember, Remember

Remember, the most difficult thing about habituation is remembering. Since you will be doing something relatively small and simple, it will be easy to forget. Typically, you will start out well, and then a few weeks later, you'll remember that you've forgotten. At that point, it is easy to give up all together. So here are some ways to help you remember over time.

Identify a time frame. In the space below, write down on what day will you start and end your habituation. In order to be effective in creating habits of virtue, you should practice your plan for an extended period of time (this workbook is based on a thirteen-week/three-month habituation period).

I will begin my habituation on: _____ (write start date)

I will end my habituation on: _____ (write end date)

Help yourself with reminder mechanisms. Reminders can be anything from a Post-It on your mirror, to a digital reminder in your calendar app. Anything works if it works for you. But it is important to set it up now. This workbook will ask you for a brief journal entry on your habituation plan at the start of each of the next thirteen weeks. If you are working with a group, your group leaders are instructed to encourage brief reporting sessions on your habituation each time you meet.

Keep a journal. You may already journal regularly. Or you may have never journaled, so this is another new habit to develop. How often you journal about your habituation plan and how you do this is entirely up to you. It might be as short as a weekly checklist ("I habituated well . . . I was distracted . . . I forgot to habituate") or as long as a few pages of self-reflection every day. You can also use this workbook to journal as you engage with the response opportunities that are provided every week. The main thing is that it is regular.

Verify

Before you write your habituation plan verify your understanding of what you are about to do.[23]

(a) The main point of a habituation plan is to generate new _____.

(b) New habits of virtue actions have the effect of shaping your _____.

(c) What does the acronym SMART stand for in relation to your habituation plan?

_____

_____

(d) As time passes, it is very easy to forget and abandon a habituation plan. This is the main challenge.   ❏ True   ❏ False

(e) How many weeks are planned in this workbook for your habituation?

_____

Act: Write Your Habituation Plan

You will now write a habituation plan to develop your chosen virtue. The examples that you have seen above illustrate that the plan does not need to be long or complex. Here is a suggested list of eight questions that might serve as your outline.

1. What is your chosen virtue? Is there also a specific vice that you have identified?

2. What kind of activities are characteristic of this virtue? Make a general list.

3. Which specific activity(ies) do you choose to repeat over the coming months?

4. How is your plan specific?

5. How is your plan measurable?

6.   How is your plan achievable?

7.   How is your plan relevant?

8.   How is your plan time bound?

Now write your plan. Take your time. Think about it carefully. Maybe draft something, sleep on it and revise it on the following day. Once you have a plan that feels right for you, write it out in the space below. A good plan is no longer than half a page, so the space should be sufficient.

My Habituation Plan:

Now that you have a habituation plan, begin practicing it this week for the first time.

⊞ Bible Study: Things Do Not Happen on Their Own

Read: Esther 4–7

This week you have developed a habituation plan as a specific choice to do something to develop your character. When you believe in God, it can be tempting to think that he will do everything and that good things will happen on their own without too much effort on your part. But that is wrong. When it comes to shaping your character, it will not happen without planning and action.

Today's story is from the book of Esther. If you are not familiar with this dramatic story about the risk of annihilation of the people of Israel at the hands of Haman, read it from the beginning.

By the time you get to chapter 4, you will see that Haman had made careful plans for evil and that he is intent on carrying them out.

But also notice that Mordecai and Esther are make corresponding plans for the good and are just as determined to carry them out. Here is what they are doing:

- Mordecai plans to involve Esther and then communicates with her (4:8).
- Esther plans to talk to the king and then makes adequate preparations, including a call to prayer for the success of her plan (4:18).
- Esther plans for her entrance to the king, and then puts on her royal robes and goes to the court of the palace (5:1).
- Esther plans for a double banquet to build anticipation (5:4–8), and then she prepares and offers the banquets.
- Esther plans to leverage the king's affection for her to save her people, and then, when the time is right, she launches a passionate plea (7:3–4).

The story ends well. The people of Israel are saved and Haman is punished. And we note that the keys to this success are intentional planning and action.

Of course there is another crucial component in this particular story, which neither Esther nor Mordecai could plan. This was what happens in chapter 6, where the king is not able to sleep and asks for the record of his reign to be brought to him. If you do not know the story, read what happens and how it sets the stage perfectly for the last part of Esther's plan.

Was God the architect behind what happens in chapter 6? We are not told. But we do know that God often steps into history to support our plans with his intervention.

Now respond: Mordecai and Esther are great examples of planning followed by action. What is one thing about Esther or Mordecai that you would like to imitate as you make plans to work on your character?

A Prayer

Lord, as I plan for virtue and make a habituation plan, may I be like Esther. May I see the need and make careful and wise plans to do something about it. And I also ask that, like you did with Esther, you may surprise me and bless my plans with your intervention.

> This week you have crafted a specific habituation plan and have
> begun to practice it. Next week you will add a second tool to
> your intensive practice, which is of character friendship.

Date completed: _____

Week 11

Character Friendship

Discover character friendship

This week you are going to engage with another tool to grow in character and virtue. But first, monitor your habituation through the habituation check below.

Habituation Check 1. This is the first week of practicing your habituation plan. For the next twelve weeks, you will find this little response box at the top of each page to help you journal and monitor your plan. Take a few moments to complete it now.

	Journal entry:
❏ I applied my habituation plan well this week	
❏ I only marginally applied my habituation plan	
❏ I forgot/was too busy to apply my habituation plan	

The Best Kind of Friendship

The cultivation of intentional character friendships is the second tool of character and virtue education (go back to Week 8 for an overview of these tools). This lesson will help you understand what character friendship is, why it is an important element in the practice of developing virtue and what you and your character friend might do in this intensive practice phase.

Let's start with a quote about friendship that comes from Aristotle:

> "Friendship is a virtue or involves virtue. Friendship is one of the most indispensable requirements of life . . . Friends are of help . . . in doing good things.[24]

Notice the last sentence: friends are of "help in doing good things."

Clearly, our friends are valuable in themselves, and we love them for their own sake, but there is also an instrumental value in friendship as they can be a help in doing good things. How is this related to your growth in character?

What Is Character Friendship?

Let us continue for a moment with Aristotle who has helpfully distinguished three types of friendships: *utility* friendships, *pleasure* friendships and *virtue* friendships. Utility friendships are those in which there is reciprocal usefulness in a relationship, such as what you may find with a good colleague at work. Pleasure friendships are those in which there is enjoyment, such as what you might find with friends with whom you share your hobbies. But then there are virtue friendships that stand above the other types. All kinds of friendship are good, all are helpful and all three may be present at the same time. But of the three, virtue friendship is the highest, because it serves the highest end in helping you do good things and become the kind of virtuous person you are meant to be. These are what we are calling "character friendships."

What exactly is a character friendship? It is a friendship that is based on the reciprocal love of each other's virtuous character, and which is expressed in the service of mutual character development.

For example, a character friend will love the virtue of diligence in your character and will want to serve and reinforce that aspect of your character so that you can be a better person. Your character friend is not trying to change you because your character is bothersome. Rather, your character friend wants to see more of the virtue of diligence in your life for your sake, in order to see you flourish as a human being and grow as a disciple of Christ.

In thinking of character friends, there are a couple of areas in which you need to be careful.

First, be careful of "friends" who have a wonderful plan to shape your life and who consider you as their personal building site! Manipulation can lurk around the corner, and this kind of "friendship" can easily become toxic. A good character friend will have input into who you are, but they will do so from the side-lines and not as the director of your life.

Second, character friendship can be risky because it involves critical input into our lives. The Roman philosopher Cicero remarks that "to graciously give and receive criticism is the mark of true friendship."[25] A character friend will be honest and tell you if there are flaws in your character. But that is something you may not like. You may prefer to be praised rather than critiqued and tend to surround yourself with friendships that are static, complacent and based on mutual admiration, rather than those that produce sparks as "iron sharpens iron." But character friendships that are at high risk of rupture will be those in which you will find the greatest help as you grow in your character.

How a Character Friend Will Help You Grow

Having seen what character friendship is, how can you expect to grow in your character through intentionally cultivating such a friendship?

Here are three things that happen as you intentionally develop character friendships:[26]

1. You will flourish in an emotional context of mutual trust. There is a unique connection of trust that happens between character friends, and this "cushion" of protection provides a sense of existential security in which vulnerability, disclosure and reception can happen. All of these are essential to grow in character.

2. You will grow as you critically dialogue over virtue. This can be conceptual dialogue where you struggle together in understanding what the virtues are and how they relate to real life. But more importantly, it can be personal, specific dialogue about virtue in each other's character which will lead to critique and an invitation to change and improve. This is why a character friend is sometimes called a critical friend.

3.   You will see yourself as never before. Character friendship provides a faithful mirror of who you are. Once again, Aristotle has put it well:

> Now we are not able to see what we are from ourselves . . . as when we wish to see our own face, we do so by looking into the mirror, in the same way when we wish to know ourselves, we can obtain that knowledge by looking at our friend.[27]

Self-assessment, such as what you have done in the Virtue Test, is a good thing but it can be delusional and short-sighted. Assessment through someone else's eyes can provide a more objective point of view as your character friends often see you better than you see yourself.

We need to be cautious and not overstate the power of character friendship in character and virtue education. All of the things listed above can happen, but that may also not happen, despite your efforts to cultivate character friends. In the coming weeks you will discover how character friendships can benefit your own growth.

Verify

Verify your understanding of character friendship.[28]

(a) Character friendship is the second tool that will be used in this workbook together with habituation.
☐ True
☐ False

(b) Friendship can be considered as "help in doing _____."

(c) What are the three kinds of friendship described by Aristotle?

_____

_____

_____

(d) Character friendship is based on the reciprocal love of each other's virtuous character.
☐ True
☐ False

(e) One of the dangers of character friendship is _____.

(f) A character friend is also a _____ friend.

Act: Who Might Your Character Friend Be?

This workbook envisions four meetings over the next twelve weeks with your character friend. You will receive guidelines on your meetings as you progress, but in general here is what you will do:

1. You will build trust by reciprocally sharing victories and failures in your character.

2. You will give account of your habituation plan. Ideally, your character friend could be someone who is also using this workbook and has their own practice plan, so the accountability is reciprocal.

3. You will reason about virtue together, discussing specific virtues and what they look like in real life.

4. You will receive critical input on your character. This is a constructive dialogue where correction is welcomed.

Who might your character friend(s) be? Next week you will receive further guidance and you will make a choice. For this week just write three or four potential names in the space below.

During this week, pray about these names, seeking guidance on who the best person might be to reach out to as a character friend.

Note: if you are going through this workbook with a group, your group leader will likely organize character friend triplets. This means that you will be assigned to regularly meet with two character friends in the coming months.

† Bible Study: A Story of Twin Souls

Read: 1 Samuel 18

This week you have thought about friendship, and the Bible is full of stories about friendship. We have stories of failed friendships (Euodia and Syntyche), rekindled friendships (Peter and Jesus), friendships that never happened (Cain and Abel) and ministry friendships (Paul and Barnabas).

But perhaps the most famous story of friendship in the Bible is the one between David and Jonathan. What can you learn from this story and how might it apply to character and virtue?

Notice, first of all, that 1 Samuel 18:1 claims that Jonathan's "soul was knit" to David. This means that a close bond was forged between them. But what made this friendship happen?

If you look carefully, you will notice that the text includes a crucial "when." This "when" helps us understand what it was that caused such a close bond. The text says "*when* David finished talking to Saul (then) Jonathan's soul was knit . . ." So the context of this friendship is the speech that David had just made to Saul concerning the defeat of Goliath (see the previous chapter 1 Samuel 17).

So this is what sparked this friendship. Jonathan sees before himself a daring man, with a crazy faith in God. And when he sees that, he sees the same virtue that was in his own character. If, in fact, you look back a few chapters to 1 Samuel 14, you will discover that Jonathan did something very similar to what David had just done with Goliath when he ventured alone with his armour-bearer into the Philistine outpost, claiming: "nothing can hinder the LORD from saving, whether by many or by few" (14:6). Jonathan was just like David: he was a daring man, with a crazy faith in God.

And it was this twinning of souls that knit the two friends together. It was the shared virtues of courage, zeal and faith in particular that forged their deep bond.

The lesson is that friendship is a twinning of souls around virtue. Or, we might say that virtue is the glue of friendship.

Now respond: The lesson from the story of David and Jonathan is that, if you want to make your friendships stronger and longer, you need the glue of virtue.

Think about your best friends (which, incidentally, should include your spouse if you are married). What important things bind you together? Do these things include virtues? Are you deeply bound to someone because you share the virtues of compassion, intellectual curiosity, or justice? Or have you recently lost or broken a friendship? Were the reasons connected to a loss of shared virtues?

Write below the name of a special friend in your life and list some of the virtues that bind you together.

A Prayer

Lord, thank you for the "Davids" in my life. Thank you for the friends with whom my soul is deeply bound. I recognize that virtue is the glue that holds us together, so grant us the grace to cultivate our character that we may continue to enjoy the gift of one to the other.

This week you have been introduced to the concept of character friendship, next week you will engage with a character friend.

Date completed: _____

Week 12

Engage a Friend

Connect with a character friend

Before you engage with the content for this week, take a moment for a habituation check.

Habituation Check 2. This is the second week of practicing your habituation plan, journal below to monitor your practice.

❑ I applied my habituation plan well this week

❑ I only marginally applied my habituation plan

❑ I forgot/was too busy to apply my habituation plan

Journal entry:

Engaging a Friend

As you continue putting your habituation plan into practice, this week you will intentionally reach out to a character friend.

You've seen how character friendship can be a powerful dynamic in your character growth. But how can you identify a character friend who will walk with you in the coming weeks?

Here are some selection criteria for a good character friend. You may already have someone in mind, but here are seven questions to further help you:

1.   **Do they know me well?** It may seem obvious, but the first question you need to ask yourself as you identify a character friend is whether they know you well. Have you spent time together in significant activities? Have you shared joys and sorrows together? Are they able to identify your greatest struggles, deepest desires and most nasty habits? Do you think of them as "soulmates"? To use the words from last week: "Does this character friend know your virtues and love your character"?

2.   **Is the friend a peer?** Although there is great benefit in character mentors (e.g. parents, teachers, pastors, etc.) and in role models that are above and beyond us (i.e. the heroes of virtue), this character growth project will focus on a friendship with someone who is like you. You are therefore looking for a soulmate, who is equal to you in social standing (i.e. not your superior), who will help you see yourself in them, and who will make you feel comfortable in genuine peer discussions that bring virtue into the realities of life. Your character friend might be a fellow student, a member in your faith community, a spouse, or a long-term friend of your same age. Ideally, it might be someone in a group who is using this workbook and is engaged in your same character growth plan.

3.   **Are we similar in virtue?** Speaking of peers, it is helpful if your character friend is similar in virtue to you. This does not mean that you must have scored equally in the Virtue Test, nor that you struggle with the same vices or have cultivated the same virtues in equal measure. It means that your character friend should be neither too bad (a fully vicious villain), nor too good (a divinely virtuous saint). Soulmates, in fact, work well in equality.

4.   **Is there mutual honesty and vulnerability in the friendship?** Has your potential character friend ever expressed good words of criticism or reproof to you? Is your relationship strong enough to tolerate mutual criticism? If this has not happened before, it may be a challenge to try to make it happen quickly now. Mutuality is also important, and the critical element of the relationship should go both ways as you both speak into each other's lives.

5. **Is my friendship considered as irreplaceable by my character friend?** This is a good question to evaluate the robustness of the relationship.

6. **Is my friendship marked by generosity?** Character friendship is about selfless giving to each other and will not work if there is a demanding spirit or a spirit of being in debt or of keeping accounts.

7. **Is there a reciprocal commitment to each other?** This may not be verbally stated, but it is important that there is some sort of covenantal relationship with your character friend. It is a commitment to each other's good, for better or for worse.

These are all great features of good character friends. But beware. As you think about who a good character friend might be, don't be too ideal or too romantic. Friendships that are genuine, dedicated, focused, exclusive and critical can be rare. In reality, most character friendships come in differing shades of intensity, and we should gratefully accept as a gift whatever is offered to us.

What if You Can't Find a Character Friend?

Most people can probably find a character friend, or at least someone who meets some of the criteria above some of the time. But what if you can't?

If you do not have character friends, a first question is whether you are humble enough to have such a friend. If, in fact, you do not welcome critical, evaluative input from others concerning the deeper parts of your soul and character, it is unlikely that you will have character friends. It might also be that you simply have never invested in this way, having found satisfaction in friendships of utility and of pleasure. If you have never practiced character friendship you are unlikely to have character friends, for we become friends by practising friendship.

There is also the chance that you are a person who is dedicated to vice and who lacks the glue of virtue in your own character. In this case, you may need to gracefully and courageously admit that you are part of the problem and begin working on your character through the other tools in this workbook. There is hope that, in time, you will become the kind of person who will have character friends.

But it is also possible that you are not the problem. It is possible that your life circumstances have isolated you. Perhaps you live in remote geographical isolation or in a foreign country. Perhaps you travel too much to settle down into any kind of permanent relationship. Perhaps there are cultural factors that stand in the way of this kind of friendship. Perhaps you are a leader who does not have access to peers. Or perhaps you have been bereaved of your closest friends. In these cases, you may need to momentarily do without the tool of character friendship in this intensive practice phase.

If you cannot find a peer character friend, it is possible to benefit from critical friendships that are "unequal." Your character friend might be your pastor, an older member of your family or a teacher that knows you well. Several of the dynamics described above will still work well, and you will enjoy the added bonus of someone who has much to give to you in terms of experience.

What if You Are Working in a Group?

This workbook can be used individually, but it is also designed to be used in group settings, such as discipleship groups, church groups or formation groups within formal theological education or non-formal training.

If you are working with such a group, what is written above is relevant, but the application mechanisms might change as follows:

1. You will not need to identify a character friend on your own. Groups of three will be formed by your group leader and you will be assigned two other participants as mutual character friends. For brevity, we will call this a Character Friend Triplet (CFT).

2. A CFT has the advantage that all of you are involved in the same character growth project and will be working through this workbook together. The other two participants of your CFT will likely meet most of the qualifications listed above, such as being peers, being similar in virtue and sharing a reciprocal commitment to character growth.

3. It is possible to be placed in a CFT with participants whom you do not know very well. In this case, take it as an opportunity to develop new friendships which may be very rewarding.

4. The group meetings will provide organized times to meet as a CFT (see the Facilitator Guidelines at the end of this workbook), so there will be some logistical help in arranging meeting times and

the character friendship dynamic will be intentionally fostered as you proceed.

All in all, if you are blessed to work with a group, the character friendship tool will benefit from the community context. If you are in doubt as to how it may work out in practice, feel free to ask your group leader for further clarification.

✅ Verify

(a) Character friendship is the second tool that you will be using in this intentional character growth project.   ❑ True ❑ False

(b) The plan will only work if I find the perfect friend.   ❑ True ❑ False

(c) This plan assumes character friendships among _____.

(d) Honesty and vulnerability among character friends is important so there can be mutual and constructive _____.

(e) If I am working in a group, I will be assigned a character friend, probably within a triplet.   ❑ True ❑ False

(f) CFT means Character Friendship Triplet.   ❑ True ❑ False

(g) If I am working on my own, this week I need to reach out and contact a character friend.   ❑ True ❑ False

---

Verify your understanding of what a character friend is and of how this will work in practice in this character growth plan.[29]

 Act: Engage a Friend

Note: If you are working as a group, you can skip this Act section. Your group leader has instructions on how to set up Character Friendship Triplets and will be doing so in your next meeting.

If you are completing this project individually, here is what you need to do:

1. Write down the name of the person you have identified as a character friend.

2. Contact them and ask them if they are available. Although a text message might suffice, a nice meal out together would be better. Here is what you might communicate:

    > *Dear _____, I have been following a programme of intentional development of my character and virtues. Part of this programme is to have a character friend. Let me explain more . . . In brief, would you be willing to walk with me in this journey? It would entail meeting up four times (every 2–3 weeks over the next 2–3 months). It might also entail some brief readings on your part (no more than twenty minutes per week). The programme will give me ideas on what to talk about when we meet, so you don't need to prepare anything. Just come along and help me as I grow.*

3. If they are available, great! Let them know that you will be reaching out to them about every two to three weeks for the next two to three months. You will be instructed on what to do with your character friend in Weeks 16, 18, 21 and 24, so you might also already put these dates in your mutual calendars.

4. If they are not available, try someone else, but try to get this done this week or else you will fall behind with the planned timetable.

If your chosen character friend is available, set up a first meeting this week. During the meeting do the following:

*   Share with them the plan you are following in this workbook, with a summary of what you have learned so far.
*   Share with them the results of your Virtue Test and your habituation plan.

- Ask your character friend to complete the Virtue Test thinking of you, and then compare the outcome with the results of your self-assessment in Week 6. Here is the QR code again from Week 6 for your convenience.

(Virtue Test)[30]

Make a few notes below on how your first meeting went.

📖 Bible Study: A Story of Good Friendship

Read: 1 Samuel 18:1–4

Last week, in speaking about character friendships, we looked at the story of David and Jonathan and of how they were similar in virtue. We return now to that story, because it is also a great example of other features in character friendship, such as those that have been described this week.

Notice the following features of David and Jonathan's friendship:

They act as peers. Although by birth Jonathan was a prince and David was a mere shepherd, Jonathan ignores this hierarchical division between them. The same is true of David, who despite his great success and popularity, always treats Jonathan with respect.

It is remarkable to note that in the peer relationship there is no envy. David is not envious of Jonathan's position and Jonathan is not envious of David's success.

There is generosity. In 18:4, we see that Jonathan takes off the robe he was wearing and gives it to David, along with his tunic, his sword, his bow and his belt. These were precious personal belongings, but Jonathan does not think twice in giving them to David without asking anything in return.

This was a concrete expression of Jonathan "loving David as himself" (18:1). A generosity that we find again later in the story when Jonathan visits David who is fleeing from his father and "helps him find strength in God" (23:16).

There is honesty and vulnerability. As the story develops in 1 Samuel 19–20 we see that the friendships between David and Jonathan encounters hardship. In particular, Jonathan's father, Saul, is consumed by envy of David's success and repeatedly tries to kill him.

Here we see honesty and vulnerability on both parts as Jonathan informs David about what is happening (20:9, 12) and admits to being relatively powerless, and David comes to Jonathan as first port of call to express his dismay and ask for advice (20:1).

There is a covenant of friendship. In 18:3 we see that Jonathan makes a covenant with David because he loves him as himself. When this covenant is put to the test, Jonathan holds to it, even if it means going against his own father, the king. He speaks well of David to Saul (19:4) and takes the side of David in the conflict (19:7; 20:2), even at the cost of bearing the rage of Saul (20:30).

In the midst of the tragedy, David and Jonathan renew their commitment to each other: "Jonathan made a covenant with the house of David, saying,

'May the LORD call David's enemies to account.' And Jonathan asks David to reaffirm his oath out of love for him, because he loved him as he loved himself" (20:16–17). As the story unfolds, we find David and Jonathan meeting again to renew their covenant (23:18).

There is emotion. Expressing emotion is a mark of deep friendship. When tragedy comes upon David, Jonathan grieves and refuses to eat (20:34). And when they finally must leave each other in order for David to save his life, they kiss each other and weep openly (20:41).

The story ends with the tragic death of Jonathan. And here David composes an intensely emotional lament: "I grieve for you, Jonathan my brother; you were very dear to me. Your love for me was wonderful, more wonderful than that of women" (2 Sam 1:26).

Now respond: The focus of this lesson has been on selecting a character friend. But what kind of character friend are you for someone else? In the box below, write down one or two of the features that David and Jonathan had as friends that you would like to be able to offer to someone else.

A Prayer

Lord may I be a friend like Jonathan. Free from envy. Generous in giving. Honest in what I do and vulnerable in what I cannot do. Faithful in my commitments and free to be emotional in my expression. And may you bless me with the gift of such friends as well.

> This week you contacted and met with your character friend
> for the first time. Next week you will begin engaging with the
> third tool in your intensive practice, which is virtue literacy.

Date completed: _____

Week 13

Improve Your Virtue Literacy

Experiment with the changing effect of virtue knowledge

Before you engage with the content for this week, take a moment for a habituation check.

Habituation Check 3. This is the third week of practicing your habituation plan, journal below to monitor your practice.

	Journal entry:
❏ I applied my habituation plan well this week	
❏ I only marginally applied my habituation plan	
❏ I forgot/was too busy to apply my habituation plan	

As you continue practicing your habituation plan with the support of your character friend, this week you will add virtue literacy as a third tool in your character growth plan.

Virtue literacy uses two powerful dynamics to shape your character: the power of knowledge and the power of emulation. Let's look at these.

The Power of Knowledge

Mere knowledge about virtue will not change you (you can, in fact, know everything about virtue and still have a vicious character). But you cannot be changed for virtue without knowledge about virtue. So, although knowledge about virtue is not a sufficient condition to be virtuous, it is a necessary condition. It is like making a cake. Flour alone is insufficient to make a good cake. But making a cake without flour is impossible.

Think of the role that knowledge and understanding about virtue have played so far in your growth plan:

- In the initial weeks you focused on understanding what character and virtue education is. In those weeks you grew in your knowledge of what virtue is, understood more about the traditions it is rooted in, and engaged your mind with words and concepts about virtue.
- Then you took the Virtue Test, and your knowledge grew more, as you began to appreciate what virtues like justice, temperance and constancy are.
- This knowledge helped you assess your own character and on that basis, you developed the habituation plan you are now working on.
- The shared knowledge about virtue is also one of the fundamental elements that holds you and your character friends together.

So you can see that knowledge about virtue appears at every step. Virtue is like a gold mine. The deeper you dig, the more you know. And the more you know, the greater the chances are that your character will be shaped by what you learn.

The Power of Emulation

Virtue literacy also shapes your character through the power of emulation.

Emulation is what happens when you watch a movie or read a book in which a character offers a particularly stirring example, and you experience a desire to be like that. So, for example, you watch *Gladiator* and want to be courageous like Maximus. You read *The Lord of the Rings* and want to be reliable like Samwise Gamgee. Or you watch a play based on *Pride and Prejudice* and walk out of the theatre determined to be more honest and loyal like Elizabeth Bennet.

These desires to be good are stirred as we allow our mind to dwell on examples of good. These examples can be of living people (e.g. our parents, a mentor or a friend), people from the past, or of imaginary people from great novels.

Since your desires have a determining effect on who you choose to be, stirring desires to emulate good examples is a powerful ally in character education.

So how exactly does emulation work? Emulation is first of all an emotion. It is actually a distressful emotion, because we perceive ourselves as being inferior to the role model that we are looking at. But after an initial distress, it can quickly become a positive emotion that arouses the desire to be equal or similar to the example that we are considering.

For emulation to work, several things need to be in place:

1) You need to choose who to observe. The first challenge is to intentionally choose positive character examples that are within reach. If, in fact, you look only at glorious heroes that you will never be able to imitate, you may experience admiration, but it will be more difficult to relate their virtues to your own experience.

2) You need to observe who you choose. Once you have identified your role models, you need to carefully observe them, read about them, watch movies or documentaries about them or engage with them in person (if they are living). You cannot, in fact, emulate what you do not know.

3) You need to recognize the qualities that you are missing and want to possess yourself. So, for example, as you read the story of Ghandi, you need to see that you are not as courageous and determined as he was in addressing injustice. And as you see that, you need to cultivate the desire to become more like him.

4) You need to avoid falling into envy or spite. Sometimes your reaction to someone that is superior to you can go in the wrong direction. Instead of wanting to emulate, you want to crush that person in order to feel less inferior. That will clearly never lead to character growth.

5) You need to move to action. Emulation moves you from knowledge to desire. But that is not enough. You should then move from desire to action. This is fundamental. Without action, you will be informed, and maybe even internally formed in your emotions and desires, but you will not be transformed in your character.

As you engage with examples of different virtues in the coming weeks, return occasionally to this check list to evaluate your growth through emulation.

9 Weeks – 9 Virtues

Here is how the tool of virtue literacy will be used in your character growth plan.

For the next nine weeks, as you continue your habituation and as you connect regularly with your character friend, you will build your virtue literacy. Here is the diagram again from Week 8 that summarizes this plan.

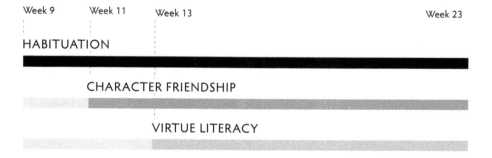

Your virtue literacy will be built around nine virtues that have been carefully selected from cardinal virtues, social virtues, personal virtues, intellectual virtues and theological virtues. Some of these were in the Virtue Test, others were not.

For each virtue you will gain knowledge of the virtue through a definition. Then you will reflect on what it looks like in your character and consider what the opposing vices might look like. Finally, you will be given a story to stimulate emulation, suggestions for areas of immediate action and a biblical exploration into that virtue.

Verify

Briefly ensure that you understand virtue literacy and how this will be used to help you grow in virtue.[31]

(a) Virtue literacy is the third tool that you will be using to build your character (alongside habituation and character friendship).   ☐ True ☐ False

(b) The first dynamic of virtue literacy is the power of _____.

(c) The second dynamic of virtue literacy is the power of _____.

(d) You cannot be changed for virtue without knowledge about virtue.   ☐ True ☐ False

(e) Emulation stirs your _____ to be virtuous as you consider examples of virtue.

(f) In the next nine weeks (as you habituate and develop your character friendship) you will also take a closer look at nine virtues as a way to build your virtue literacy.   ☐ True ☐ False

Act: Your Favourite Character

You have been given a couple of examples above of characters in movies and books that inspire emulation. Here is a chance to make this more personal. In the box below, respond to the following:

- What is the name of one of your favourite characters in a movie or book?
- Can you name the virtue that this character demonstrates?
- In what way do you feel the desire to be like them?

Emulation is one of the educational effects of reading or preaching the Bible. As your imagination engages with the stories of Aaron, Daniel and Stephen, your desires should be stirred to become more supportive, wise and courageous. In the box below, write the name of one character in the Bible who inspires emulation in you, and name the virtue that you wish to imitate.

But emulation can also be negative, and the stories like the ones of Cain and Achan should stir your desires to not be envious or greedy. In the box below, write the name of a Bible character whose vices you are determined not to imitate.

Bible Study: Focusing Your Mind

Read: Philippians 4:8

This week you have seen the power of virtue knowledge and emulation. The brief Bible study below deals with a text on emulation and on the importance of virtue literacy. In the text we find an object, an action and an outcome.

The **object** of the text is a list of well-known virtues:

- truthfulness (*alēthē*)
- nobility in character (*semnos*)
- justice (*dikaia*)
- purity (*hagna*)
- pleasing and with a good reputation (*prosphilē*)
- kindness and being full of grace (*euphēma*)

At the end of the list, Paul adds "anything that is excellent and praiseworthy." Here, he notably chooses the words *aretē*, which is the Greek word for virtue (excellent), and the word *prosphilē*, which means acceptable and pleasing.

So the virtues are the main object of this text.

The **action** of the text rotates around a key verb. *Focus your mind* on these virtues. To focus your mind can mean many things, including meditating on virtue, reading about virtue, reasoning about virtue and evaluating the importance and force of virtue.

So you need to engage your mind with these virtues.

This can be done in many ways, like writing out definitions of the virtues, working out what they look like in real-life situations, evaluating their importance in your life or reading stories about these virtues.

The **outcome** of the text is to have the peace of God. And here is a revolutionary lesson. Paul is telling us that the key to finding deep peace is in occupying our mind with the knowledge of virtue. In other words, as we "model our way of life" (Phil 4:9) on thinking about virtue, our character will be shaped, we will experience a life of flourishing and we will find inner peace.

Now respond: In the Act section above you have thought about virtue in Bible characters. Here is a further exercise meant to focus your mind on virtues in Bible characters. What characters/stories in the Bible might be associated with the virtues below?

Try to complete the following list (the first one is provided). There are no right or wrong answers, so think freely based on your familiarity with

Bible stories. If you have only just begun reading the Bible, you might want to complete this exercise with someone else.

(Example) Truthfulness . . . *when the prophet Micaiah gets slapped in the face for telling king Jehoshaphat the truth about the upcoming defeat in battle* (1 Kings 22).

Nobility in character _____

_____

Justice _____

_____

Purity _____

_____

Pleasing and with a good reputation _____

_____

_____

Kindness and being full of grace _____

_____

Focusing on these stories can lead to emulation. Is there one character of those you have just listed that you feel particularly drawn to? Who do you want to be more like?

A Prayer

Lord, help me focus my mind on virtue. I admit that my mind is so easily focused on other things. Grant me your peace as I focus on that which is true, whatever is noble, whatever is right, whatever is pure, whatever is lovely, whatever is admirable, if anything is excellent or praiseworthy. And, in particular, help me to be more like _____ (name the character you feel drawn to).

> This week you have learnt more about virtue literacy as the third tool that will be used in your character growth plan. Next week you will begin building your virtue literacy around a first virtue, the virtue of humility.

Date completed: _____

Week 14

Being Humble

See this entry/exit virtue in your life

Before you engage with the content for this week, take a moment for a habituation check.

Habituation Check 4. This is the fourth week of practicing your habituation plan, journal below to monitor your practice.

	Journal entry:
❏ I applied my habituation plan well this week	
❏ I only marginally applied my habituation plan	
❏ I forgot/was too busy to apply my habituation plan	

A Humble Start

In the coming weeks you will focus on specific virtues, defining what they look like, understanding what the opposite vices look like and seeing examples that inspire emulation. This will help you grow in character.

Your journey into virtue literacy begins with *humility* because it is a particular virtue. It can be considered, in fact, as a sort of entry/exit virtue to the rest of the virtues. It represents the entrance door to developing virtuous character because without humility you will never feel the need to grow in any other virtue. But it is also the potential exit point, because once you have done well in other virtues, you may become proud and undermine all the rest.

The theologian and monk John Cassian wrote a lot about virtue in the fifth century and his writings on virtue were considered "essential" Christian texts. He developed what has become known as the *Tree of Virtue*, whose top branches feature the theological virtues of *faith*, *hope* and *love*. These hover over the branches of *counsel*, *prudence*, *fortitude*, *patience*, *piety*, *justice*, *meekness* and *temperance*. But the roots of the tree are found in the virtue of *humility*, about which he wrote: "No structure of virtue can possibly be raised in our soul unless, first, the foundations of true humility are laid in our heart."[32] You need humility before you can achieve any other virtue. Only if you are humble will you recognize your need to grow. If you are not humble, no methodology or practice plan will be able to help you.

So, ask yourself, Am I humble?

Is the Virtue of Humility in Your Character?

To assess your own humility, you first need to understand what humility is. And here there are some common misconceptions, the most common of which is that humility always entails complete self-abasement and an under-estimation of your own worth. That is wrong.

The theologian Stanley Hauerwas offers a lovely description of humility as a correct assessment of yourself that depends on the gratitude for the life that you've been given.[33]

Humility is therefore a correct assessment of yourself. It is seeing yourself as you really are, neither too big, nor too small, but just the right size in each given situation.

But humility is also inextricably linked with gratitude, which is the recognition of what you have been given and for which you know you cannot take the praise. Gratitude can be for your family heritage, for mentors and friends, for life experiences and for the work of God in your life that has graced you with abilities, talents and opportunities.

Humility can express itself in many ways.

- It can be a disposition of comfortableness with yourself, that means that you do not always feel the need to talk about your achievements and abilities and that you do not always think of yourself. As C. S.

Lewis suggests, "True humility is not thinking less of yourself, but thinking of yourself less."[34]

- It can be an admission of your ignorance and deficiencies, which means that you do not mind recognizing that you do not know everything and that you are not perfect.
- It can be submission to just authorities, which means that you are not always giving the orders but are also willing to be led.
- It can be respect of your traditions, which means that you are working against the malignant vices of exasperated individualism and self-assertion to embrace your identity in a wider community.
- It can be the attribution of credit and rights to those around you, which means that you are thankful.
- It can also be an existential awareness of your own finitude, which means that you embrace the fragility of your own life.

The list could go on. Appropriate humility is meant to restrain your arrogance, gently call your efforts into doubt, curtail your infinite appetite for recognition and make you smaller in order to enlarge your world.

But don't forget that humility and modesty are also the source of self-confidence and pugnacious living. Humility is not just about "lowering" an inflated self-esteem. Humility should also be a positive assessment of yourself that leads to being rightfully "big" in given circumstances. A truly humble person knows what they are good at, does not continually exercise in self-abasement, is free to receive gratitude for hard effort and rejoices in legitimate achievements.

The Opposing Vices

As you build your knowledge of the virtues, it is helpful to look at the opposing vices. Some of these will be vices of defect (not enough humility) and some will be vices of excess (too much humility).

The most evident vice of humility-by-defect is *pride*, along with its awful cousins of *arrogance, shamelessness* and *false modesty*. Pride is the first of the capital vices. Augustine suggests that pride is "love gone bad" for it fails its right purpose which is to love God and your neighbour. Pride is when you love yourself with all your heart and use your neighbour to nourish your self-love.

The mythological story of Narcissus is emblematic of pride, as the beautiful young boy becomes infatuated by his own reflected image in a pool of water, but he falls into it and drowns. In the *Divine Comedy*, Dante imagines the proud as being punished by carrying enormous rocks that do not allow them to stand straight, bending them after death for what they have refused to do in life. Ultimately, he places the proud in a swamp where they are isolated forever in their own grandeur.

But humility can also have vices-by-excess. Yes, paradoxically, you can be too humble! Humility, as we've seen, empowers you to wear your legitimate abilities and achievements in a spirit of modesty. So let us repeat this one more time: humility is not *self-abasement*, where you continually undermine your true achievements. It is not *self-effacement*, where you wipe yourself out as if all the good that you are and have done is of no worth. It is not *self-replacement*, where you attribute achievements that legitimately come from your own efforts to someone else.

A Story of Humility

The story is told of Nelson Mandela, who always made his own bed, no matter where he travelled. He stayed once in Shanghai in a very fancy hotel, in which Chinese hospitality required that guests always be served by someone who was assigned to clean rooms and provide food. For guests to do these things on their own was regarded as an insult.

In Shanghai Mandela was advised, "Please don't make your own bed, because there's this custom here." And he said, "Call the cleaning personnel and bring them to me." So the hotel manager brought the ladies who would be cleaning the room, and he graciously expressed his appreciation to them and explained that he was in the habit of making his own bed, and that they should not feel insulted by him doing so.

Here Mandela gives us a double example of humility. First, he did not use his status or economic advantage to demand or expect the service of others. Making his own bed was a gesture of gratitude for his privilege and of appreciation of the work of others. But Mandela also didn't want to hurt people's feelings. He never really cared about what great people thought of him, but he did care about what small people thought of him.[35]

Do you feel an internal tug to want to be more like Mandela? Have you ever made your bed in a hotel? When you go to a restaurant, how do you treat the waiters? If you are a pastor in a church, do you expect the best parking place? If you are training for the ministry, are you doing so to gain status and be served by others?

These are difficult questions, but they can be of great help.

If this brief lesson on humility has generated a desire to be humbler, then be encouraged. Virtue literacy is working in you and is producing a positive effect.

✅ Verify

Before proceeding, verify your understanding of the virtue of humility.[36]

(a) If you are not humble, you will never grow in other virtues.

❑ True
❑ False

(b) Humility can be described as a correct _____ of yourself.

(c) Humility always comes with _____ for what you have received.

(d) Humility is not just about lowering an inflated self-esteem.

❑ True
❑ False

(e) A vice-by-defect of humility is _____.

(f) A vice-by-excess of humility is _____.

(g) You are now engaging with all three tools for character development: habituation, character friendship and virtue literacy.

❑ True
❑ False

👥 Act: Humility Check

How did you score in the Virtue Test in the virtue of humility? (You may need to consult your results again from Week 6.) Do you identify with the descriptions given above of humility in your character? If so, well done, you are a humble person (and recognizing humility does not make you lose it).

But do some of the opposing vices also describe you? In particular, did the example of Mandela about not using his status to be served move something in you?

Here is the action point for this week. Identify a small privilege that you benefit from because of your status (e.g. someone makes your bed, your secretary brings you coffee, your mother washes the dishes). As an act of humility, do two things: (1) express your gratitude to the person who normally serves you and (2) give up your privilege for this week (or longer). If it is possible, consider serving the person who normally serves you (e.g. bring coffee to your secretary).

In the box below, write what you did and how it went.

As you perform this action this week, be thinking about how Jesus demonstrated humility in washing his disciples' feet.

† Bible Study: *Ecce Ancilla Domini*

Read: Luke 1:38, 44–45

There are many stories of humility in the Bible, and this week you are going to consider the story of Mary, when she is told that she is to be the mother of the Messiah and she defines herself as "the Lord's servant." The beautiful Latin expression that translates this is *Ecce ancilla Domini*.

Think of it. Mary was a privileged young woman. Of all the privileges that God has given humanity, none is comparable to the privilege of bearing the Son of God and nurturing him into the world. If anyone could have been proud, it was Mary. But this young woman gives us a deep lesson in humility.

Here is what we learn from her reply:

1) "I am a servant." Mary sees privilege as a service. She is a *doloue* (Greek). An *ancilla* (Latin). A servant. This is what love of God and love of our neighbour should look like. To be privileged means to serve others and not build your own fame.

2) "May the Lord do to me." Mary sees herself as a grateful beneficiary of God's work. It is not "I will do," but "God will do" something through me.

3) "Others will call me blessed." Notice that she does not say that others "will say I'm great" or others "will notice how good I am at this." She is simply grateful to God and aims at being called blessed because the Lord has done great things.

Are you like Mary? Do you see yourself as a channel through which great abilities, privileges and leadership roles flow past without you holding onto them for your own self-grandeur?

Notice that this particular story tells of a moment in which Mary is completely passive and the Lord does everything. But it is not always so. You are often called to do things and to "collaborate" with the grace of God. In these cases you should learn to recognize your own work alongside the work of God. You should not be awkward in your efforts to be unduly humble. If you have worked hard, mended a relationship, completed a project, or improved your character through intentional habituation, enjoy a legitimate sense of joy and accomplishment in what is well done.

Now respond: What privileges do you have in your life? What things do you do well? Write one privilege or thing that you do well in the box below, and then write how this may be of service to others.

A Prayer

Lord, may I not be among the proud whom you will scatter, but among the humble who are lifted up by you. Teach me to be a servant who wishes to be called blessed. Teach me also to take rightful ownership for the things I have done and to find deep joy for the things that you will reward me for.

This week you have built your virtue literacy by focusing on the virtue of humility. Next week you will look at the virtue of temperance.

Date completed: _____

Week 15

Being Temperate

See this cardinal virtue in your life

As you stay on track with your habituation plan, this week you will build your virtue literacy and meet with your character friend. But first, take a moment for a habituation check.

Habituation Check 5. This is the fifth week of practicing your habituation plan, journal below to monitor your practice.

❑ I applied my habituation plan well this week ❑ I only marginally applied my habituation plan ❑ I forgot/was too busy to apply my habituation plan	Journal entry:

Combining the Right Proportions

This week you will allow your mind to dwell on the virtue of *temperance*. Let's start by defining what temperance is. In English, the word "temperance" comes from the Latin *temperare*, which literally means "to combine in the right proportions." It was used, for example, to describe the right combination of colours for an artist, the right proportions of herbs in a recipe and the right combination of warm and cold water.

Consider each of these examples further. Imagine an artist who desires to paint a deep blue sea but adds too much black to the palette. This will generate a horribly dark result. Or imagine a cook who uses the amount of garlic needed for 100 portions of sauce into 2 portions. The result would be distasteful. And when you take a shower, how important is it to get the right proportions of hot and cold water and thus avoid an "intemperate" shower?

Temperance is the virtue that keeps good things from going overboard and that maintains the right proportions. When it comes to your character, there are things that need to be combined in the right proportions. Having fun, for example, is a good thing, but it needs to be proportioned with responsibility. Orderliness is a wonderful virtue, but it needs to be proportioned with flexibility. Spending your money on entertainment is great, but it needs to be proportioned with wise savings to pay your bills.

Temperance is needed in every area of your life: you need temperance in your relationships, in following your desires, in your sexuality, in your work habits, in your political involvement, in handling your emotions, in making choices, in religious devotion, in speaking, in eating and drinking, in enjoying art, in practicing sports, and so on.

Is the Virtue of Temperance in Your Character?

How do you know if the virtue of temperance is at work in your character? Here is what it looks like. If you are temperate:

- You will be able to govern yourself with the help of reason and your actions and words will not be driven by passion, desire and impulse alone.
- You will be content with your state and you will be inwardly at rest.
- You will be able to tame your impulses and appetites and you will be able to say "no" or "enough" when necessary.

There is a rich cluster of synonyms for temperance. *Moderation* is the virtue that regulates your attraction to pleasure and balances your use of the good things in creation. *Self-control* is the virtue whereby you are the owner of yourself and are able to tame your will to produce right action. *Self-discipline* is the virtue that allows you to "force" yourself to do what you do not want to do, or not to do what you might be tempted to do. *Abstinence* is the virtue of governing your passions and doing without that which is out of proportion.

Meekness is an interesting virtue that is not usually associated with temperance. We think, in fact, of a meek person as a person who is quiet and remissive. The true meaning of meekness, however, has to do with being self-possessed in mitigating your anger. Meekness is therefore exercised in the presence of evil, and it is the middle ground between the vices of *irascibility* on the one hand and *indifference* on the other.

Do these words describe you? If so, well done, you are a temperate person.

The Opposing Vices

There are also several vices that oppose the virtue of temperance. These can be divided in the vices of defect and of excess.

The vices of defect are those where you do not have enough temperance. These are the vices of *licentiousness* and *self-indulgence* where nothing is ever denied, and of *lust* where there are no limits placed on sexual impulses. The capital sin of *gluttony* is also a lack of temperance and can be seen in having no control in your relationship with food and drink, either indulging in too much of it, unduly depriving yourself of it or becoming extremely sophisticated in what you will or will not eat.

The vices of excess are those where you have too much temperance. It is, in fact, possible to go too far in trying to get the right proportions. This can be seen for example in the vices of continual *self-denial* or unwarranted *asceticism* in which all pleasure is avoided. Or when the ambition of having total control over your life becomes the vice of *obsession*, that can lead to personality disorders such as that of compulsion-obsession (OCD).

Do any of these describe you? If they do, and if your score in the Virtue Test was low in the virtue of temperance, then perhaps you should work on this virtue in your character.

A Story of Intemperance

Today's story is about King Midas. Ancient Greek mythology tells us about this king who was very rich and had more gold than anyone else in the world. And yet, he was deeply unhappy because he always wanted more.

The only other joy in his life was his beautiful daughter Marygold. She, incidentally, cared nothing about gold.

One day a stranger (the god Dionysus) appeared to King Midas and offered him the gift of turning anything he touched into gold. The king greedily accepted this gift and went about touching everything. Sure enough, to his delight, everything he touched turned to gold. But the gift could not be turned off. When he tried to eat, his food turned to gold. And when he tried to drink, his wine turned to liquid gold.

And so, the tragedy began to unfold. Shortly after Midas had walked through his garden, turning leaves and flowers into gold, his daughter Marygold ran to him distraught because she had discovered that the beautiful roses in her garden had been turned into the cold metal. The king offered words of comfort, but she, unaware of the new danger her father represented, threw her arms around him. As he inadvertently touched her, the beautiful Marygold was also turned into a lifeless statute of gold.

And so the king, who lacking temperance sought to have everything, in the end lost everything.

✅ Verify

Revise and verify your understanding of the virtue of temperance.[37]

(a) Temperance means finding the right proportions of various aspects of your life.
❑ True
❑ False

(b) Write a synonym for temperance (even in your own language). _____

_____

(c) Our passions, desires and impulses are good things, but we should also be governed by

_____.

(d) Temperance includes being able to say _____.

(e) Self-control when you are angry is the virtue of _____.

(f) Which of the opposing vices to temperance do you struggle with most? _____

_____

👥 Act: Engage Your Character Friend

You may recall that in Week 12 you reached out to a character friend as part of your plan for practice. This week you need to organize a time to meet with your friend for a second time.

Write the time/date of your meeting in the box below:

If you are working with a group, a meeting with your Character Friend Triplet (CFT) will be organised this week, so you do not need to plan this separately.

Here is a suggested outline for your time together:

1. Give account of your habituation plan.

2. Talk about the virtue of temperance that you have considered this week. Share your victories and failures. Discuss the story of King Midas, reasoning on its meaning and applying it to your lives. Don't forget to ask your friend for critical input around temperance in your life.

3. If time allows, do the same with the virtue of humility that you considered last week.

Write some brief notes in the box below describing your meeting with your character friend.

✝ Bible Study: Two Men on the Temperance Spectrum

Read: Genesis 39 and 2 Samuel 11

There are many stories in the Bible that speak about temperance. Here we will look at two of them, one as an example of virtue and the other as an example of vice.

Joseph: an example of temperance. The main character in Genesis 39 is Joseph. He is at a point in his life where, after many difficulties, things are finally taking a positive turn. After being sold by his brothers as a slave, he has been brought to a place of status in the house of the Egyptian dignitary Potiphar. But then something happens. Because he was well built and handsome (39:6) Potiphar's wife laid her eyes on him and did all she could to go to bed with him.

This illustrates the context in which you may need temperance:

- You may be coming out of a difficult situation and feel that you deserve something.
- You are presented with an opportunity for pleasure, but you know that it is a "wrong combination." Potiphar's wife, in Joseph's own words, was "withheld from him" and did not belong to him (39:9).
- Pleasure is there for you without any apparent negative consequences. Potiphar's wife, in the story, offers herself to him "when there is no one in the house" (39:11). The temptations of intemperance are strongest when you are convinced that no one will see or know.

But here is what character with temperance looks like:

1. Joseph governs himself through reason. His actions are not driven by desire but by the reflection that to take Potiphar's wife would be an act of wickedness against both Potiphar and God (39:9).

2. Joseph is content with his own state, recognizing that "no one in this house is greater than I am" (39:9).

3. Joseph is able to tame appetites, meaning that he is able to say no when necessary. The text never says that Joseph did not like Potiphar's wife, but it says that even as she insisted "day after day, he refused to go to bed with her" (39:10).

4. Joseph acts to support his self-control. At times, temperance takes control-before-the-time, and can mean planning to avoid situations

where we know control is more difficult. Here we see a notable little clause, "he refused to even be with her" (39:10).

Even though Joseph's character holds firm, sadly the story does not end well for him. Potiphar's wife accuses him unjustly and he is sent back to jail. And here is an additional lesson for us. Good character does not always yield immediate success, and virtue does not always improve our circumstances. We are virtuous because it is right, not because it leads us to be better off.

David: an example of intemperance. The story of David and Bathsheba is familiar and is a sad example of the vice of intemperance. If you do not know this story, read it in 2 Samuel 11. We will not examine it in detail, but just note the similarities and differences with the story of Joseph.

In both stories, the circumstances are similar. There is an opportunity for pleasure without any apparent consequences. The difference is that, while Joseph shows us what temperance looks like, David exhibits a character of intemperance and yields to pleasure.

We also note that David does not govern himself through reason. His actions are driven by desire alone. He is not content with his own state and wants more than what he already has. He does not tame his appetites and does not choose to say no when necessary.

David's intemperance has dramatic consequences as the story unfolds. The same is true for us, as we cannot predict the outcomes of our lack of temperance.

Now respond: Is there something in either of these two stories of temperance that relates to your own experience? Write this down briefly below.

A Prayer

Lord, may I be like Joseph. Temperate in my actions, words and choices in all circumstances because it is the right thing to do. And help me to not be like David, who relaxed and fooled himself that his good track record in the past exempted him from the ongoing exercise of virtue.

> This week you applied all three tools of your practice plan and focused on the virtue of temperance. Next week you will be looking at the virtue of courage.

Date completed: _____

Week 16

Being Courageous

See this cardinal virtue in your life

As you continue to work on your habituation plan, meet with your character friend and build your virtue literacy, you are a little less than half way through your intensive practice stage. Well done. As usual, begin this week with a habituation check.

Habituation Check 6. This is the sixth week of practicing your habituation plan, journal below to monitor your practice.

	Journal entry:
❏ I applied my habituation plan well this week	
❏ I only marginally applied my habituation plan	
❏ I forgot/was too busy to apply my habituation plan	

Pursuing True Courage

This week you will focus on the cardinal virtue of *courage*.

Courage is necessary because the world is a frightening place at every stage of life. Childhood is frightening. Teenage years are frightening. Adulthood and old age are also frightening. We fear for our health. We fear for our safety. We fear we will not be accepted. We fear failure. We fear for the economy. We fear war. We fear famine. We fear difficult relationships. We fear for our jobs. We fear betrayal. We fear death.

It is these fears that make courage so important.

Courage helps you as a child as you learn how to ride a bicycle. Courage takes you through the challenges of education. Courage enables you to make difficult decisions at work and sustains you as you try to innovate and try what has never been done before. Courage allows you as a mother to stand up and protect your child from bullying. Courage accompanies you in having difficult marital conversations. Courage gives you the will to fight your diseases. And eventually courage will be what you need as your life comes to an end.

If you are to live fully in the presence of the fears of life, courage is an essential virtue.

Is the Virtue of Courage in Your Character?

The virtue of courage is best described as taming your will to do what is good in the face of legitimate fears. Read that again and let it soak in.

Note carefully. Courage is not absence of fear, but right action in the presence of fear. There are times, in fact, when the feeling of fear is legitimate and when it is right to be terrified of what is before us. But what we should not allow is that fear paralyze us. That is, in fact, the natural effect of fear. Fear stops us. Fear keeps us from facing challenges. Fear makes us retreat from right action for the sake of safety.

The key difference is between feeling fear, which is inevitable, and not doing anything because of fear, which is wrong. And that is where you need courage. That is where your will must be tamed to do what is good and right.

Jesus felt fear in Gethsemane, but that did not stop him from going to the cross. Moses felt fear before Pharaoh, but that did not stop him from demanding freedom for the people of Israel. David surely felt fear before Goliath, but he picked up his sling anyway and went out to fight the giant.

The virtue of courage is found in your character when you face fearful situations that are larger than you are, and, despite those fears, you bend your will to do your duty. The key is not that you never experience fear. The key is that fear does not control you.

The Opposing Vices

The main vice-by-defect that opposes courage is *cowardice*, which is when you allow your fears to dominate you. A coward is one who forfeits doing what is right in order to avoid pain. When you are a coward, you shrink your life and give up on living fully. The bicycle is there, but you never ride it.

Unreliability is also associated with cowardice and can be a devastating vice in your relationships. A person who is unreliable, in fact, is one that makes promises but does not keep them when difficulties arise. If you are unreliable, those around you will be continually let down. Courage will improve your relationships by helping you maintain your course despite adverse winds of circumstance.

Discouragement can also become a vice. Think carefully about this word in light of the above. What does it mean to be dis-couraged? It means that adverse circumstances have overcome you, overwhelmed you and taken away your energy to do what is right. You have lost courage. Fear has paralyzed you. Discouragement can be a common experience in your walk of discipleship and Christian service, which is why developing the virtue of courage is so important.

Another, perhaps unexpected, vice that is related to courage is the *repression of wrath*. Yes, you read that correctly, not the vice of wrath, but the vice of suppressing wrath. Sometimes, as Christians, we feel that anger is always wrong and that it must always be blocked. But that is not the case. The emotion of anger is an important ally to courage. Feelings of indignation and of aggression against the forces that are threatening your loved ones, for example, will give you the strength to oppose them. When, in 1 Samuel 17:46 David yells back at Goliath "I'll strike you down and cut off your head!" it is evident that he was feeling emotions of strong anger against Goliath. And this righteous anger helped him find the courage to fight. So don't always repress anger.

It is also possible, however, to have too much courage, which means that you do not have sufficient fear of the things that you should fear. There are things that we need to fear, in order to remain safe and be prudent. If you are driving on the edge of a precipice, it is right to feel fear because that will make you careful. So do not think that being a disciple of Jesus means to be fearless. The vices of *imprudence, rashness, foolhardiness* and *recklessness* describe those who refuse to fear anything. And these are vices that need to be reined in by a correct expression of courage.

Do any of these vices describe you? If they do, and if your score in the Virtue Test was low in this virtue, then you may need to work on the virtue of courage in your character.

A Story of Courage in *The Lord of the Rings*

The Lord of the Rings by J. R. R. Tolkien has earned itself a rightful place among the great books of the world. And one of the things that turns this fascinating story into a true epic is the depiction of virtue in its characters.

Courage is one of the prominent virtues in *The Lord of the Rings*. It marks every step of the way as the Company of the Ring carries out its mission to destroy the Ring of Power in the face of terrifying forces of evil. What is remarkable is the characters with greatest courage in *The Lord of the Rings* are neither fearless nor inherently courageous. Tolkien does not choose a Hollywood Hero view, where courage is something that "some people have" because they are big, strong and full of superpowers. Rather, Tolkien shows that real people, who are small, insignificant and full of fragilities can face great fears and "find courage within" to do the right thing. For him, courage is not a capacity but a repeated choice.

Nowhere do we see this more clearly than in the small hobbits who, despite their weakness and insignificance, rise to deeds of unthinkable courage. Frodo at Rivendell faces the Nazgul (whose power lies in fear), vowing that they would have "neither the Ring nor me!" Samwise blinds the spider Shelob with the Phial of Galadriel to save Frodo. And Merry deserves the praise of Aragorn who claims of him: "He knows not to what end he rides; yet if he knew, he would still go on."

Of course, some of Tolkien's characters have amazing capacities, like Gandalf, Aragorn, Legolas or Gimli. But their courage is most clearly expressed in situations they would have rather avoided, and in which they choose to accomplish their mission for the good of their people, of their companions and eventually of all Middle Earth. For them, despite their capacities, courage means facing the unknown even while flinching, unsteady or downright terrified.[38]

If you have never read *The Lord of the Rings* or watched the movie trilogy by Peter Jackson, this is a great exercise in virtue literacy.

✅ Verify

Complete the small test below to summarize some main points about courage.[39]

(a) Courage is doing what is right in the face of legitimate _____.

(b) Feeling fear is a natural part of life.
❑ True
❑ False

(c) When we are overcome by difficult circumstances and feel paralyzed, we say that we are

_____.

(d) Anger is always wrong.
❑ True
❑ False

(e) The main vice-by-defect of courage is _____.

(f) A vice-by-excess of courage is _____.

(g) In *The Lord of the Rings*, the most courageous characters are weak and insignificant

_____.

Act: Perform an Act of Courage

The exercise for this week is very simple. Do something in the face of something you fear. Follow the following four steps.

1) Name a fear that you have. This could be anything from saying hello to a new neighbour, to driving your car in traffic or taking a trip to an unknown country. Write this in the box below.

2) Now name what this fear is stopping you from doing. What is the right, or normal thing, that you are not doing because of this particular fear? Write this in the box below.

3) Now write in the box the right thing that you will do this week despite this fear. Be specific.

Verify

Complete the small test below to summarize some main points about courage.[39]

(a) Courage is doing what is right in the face of legitimate _____.

(b) Feeling fear is a natural part of life.
❑ True
❑ False

(c) When we are overcome by difficult circumstances and feel paralyzed, we say that we are

_____.

(d) Anger is always wrong.
❑ True
❑ False

(e) The main vice-by-defect of courage is _____.

(f) A vice-by-excess of courage is _____.

(g) In *The Lord of the Rings*, the most courageous characters are weak and insignificant

_____.

Act: Perform an Act of Courage

The exercise for this week is very simple. Do something in the face of something you fear. Follow the following four steps.

1) Name a fear that you have. This could be anything from saying hello to a new neighbour, to driving your car in traffic or taking a trip to an unknown country. Write this in the box below.

2) Now name what this fear is stopping you from doing. What is the right, or normal thing, that you are not doing because of this particular fear? Write this in the box below.

3) Now write in the box the right thing that you will do this week despite this fear. Be specific.

4)   Finally, record briefly how things worked out. Did you do the right thing in overcoming your fear? How did you feel as you did so? How did you feel afterwards?

† Bible Study: Being strong and courageous

Read: Deuteronomy 31:7–8

The virtue of courage is at the heart of one of the core episodes of the Old Testament when the people of Israel conquer the promised land.

In Deuteronomy 31 the people of Israel have come out of Egypt, travelled through the desert, and are preparing to conquer their own land. At this crucial juncture, there is a major challenge ahead of them, and Moses encourages them to be "strong and courageous" (31:6).

These same words are repeated to Moses's successor Joshua: "Be strong and courageous, for you must go with this people into the land that the LORD swore to their ancestors to give them, and you must divide it among them as their inheritance. The LORD himself goes before you and will be with you; he will never leave you nor forsake you. Do not be afraid; do not be discouraged" (31:7–8).

Notice five things in this text:

1)   The virtue of courage is bundled together with the virtue of strength. You cannot be courageous without being strong in the face of your fears and challenges.

2)   Courage is always associated with action, and not necessarily with sentiment. Joshua is told to *go* with the people into the land . . . And *going* is an action verb that can be carried out with the will, even if the emotions do not align.

3) Courage is rooted in the promises of God. It was God who had promised the land, so Joshua's courage was well founded and not misdirected to wrong ends.

4) Courage is rooted in the presence of God. Whatever fearful circumstances Joshua might have faced he could count on the presence of the Almighty.

5) The vices that hinder courage are fear and discouragement. As we've seen in this lesson, fear itself is not the problem as much as its paralyzing effects. Discouragement, on the other hand, drains our motivation and leads to inaction. In both cases, courage in our character helps us to do the right thing.

How did things work out for Joshua? If we read further in the story, we find that Joshua's character turned out indeed to be courageous, and he led the people of Israel to face the giants in the promised land.

It is interesting to note that courage did not come then and there to Joshua. This virtue was not a divine flash of endowment. It was, instead, the fruit of his character that had been shaped over time. Look for a moment at Numbers 13 and 14, where we read a story that had happened years before. It is the episode of the Israelite spies that were sent to explore the promised land, and Joshua was one of them. As you may recall, whereas the other spies were paralyzed by the fear of the walled cities, Joshua and Caleb demonstrated courage. They encouraged the people to trust in the Lord and not be afraid for God was with them (Numbers 14:9). Courage was already at work then. The lesson is that character is not born in one day but is habituated over time.

Now respond: Do you struggle with discouragement? How does the story of Joshua help you? Which of the five things in the text speak to you in particular?

A Prayer

Lord, in the face of my fears and challenges, help me to act and do the right things with the strength of Joshua. Make your promises clear to me and allow me to feel your presence by faith. Remove from me fear and discouragement that I may do your will.

> This week you have built your virtue literacy by focusing on the virtue of courage. Next week you will look at the virtue of justice.

Date completed: _____

Week 17

Being Just

See this cardinal virtue in your life

This week you will focus on the cardinal virtue of justice and meet again with your character friend. Before you engage with the content for this week, take a moment as usual for a habituation check.

Habituation Check 7. This is the seventh week of practicing your habituation plan, journal below to monitor your practice.

	Journal entry:
❏ I applied my habituation plan well this week	
❏ I only marginally applied my habituation plan	
❏ I forgot/was too busy to apply my habituation plan	

The Domains of Justice

In the last two weeks you have seen the "cardinal" virtues of *temperance* and *courage*. This week you will consider a third cardinal virtue: *justice* (you will have to wait until Week 23 for the final cardinal virtue of *prudence*). You may recall that the word "cardinal" is used for the four virtues that are considered "hinges" on which all the other virtues turn. Surely, these virtues are among the most important in your character as a disciple.

It is difficult to overstate the all-embracing nature of the virtue of justice. It is the virtue which regulates the relationships between living beings and is both simple and incredibly complex at the same time.

The virtue of justice can be broadly thought of in two different domains: communal justice (collective) and character justice (individual) which you will now consider.

Communal Justice

Justice is first of all a communal affair, and political philosophers have written volumes on how societies should be justly arranged. Communal justice applies to all kinds of communities, including work environments, schools, families and faith-based communities. Anywhere humans live collectively, justice is needed to regulate their relations.

Communal justice, however, applies foremost to good government, and this week you are going to reflect on this virtue in a slightly different way by examining the 1338 fresco by Ambrogio Lorenzetti entitled *Allegory of Good Government* (found in the city hall of the Italian city of Siena). This fresco is a graphic illustration of the complexities of communal justice. Scan the QR code below now to view it as you read the explanations below.

(*Allegory of Good Government* – Wikimedia)[40]

Start on the far left of the fresco, where you should be able to see a representation of *Justice* as a woman dressed in burgundy and with a crown on her head. Have you found her? She is holding a set of scales that are administered by two angels. The angels are performing acts of commutative justice (you can see one man being decapitated and another one crowned) and distributive justice (the angel is providing two merchants with measuring instruments). Notice that Justice is looking up to *Wisdom*, who is holding a book to provide guidance.

Just below Justice, see if you can find *Concord* who is depicted as a woman dressed in grey and gold. She has a shaving plane in her hand, as a symbol of equality and of the need to level out civil conflicts. Notice that there is a rope that links Concord and Justice to each other and to the twenty-four citizens who represent the community of the city of Siena. The rope then joins the Commune, who sits on a throne (dressed in green and gold and holding a shield), and represents the city government.

Hovering over the Commune are the three theological virtues; *Faith*, *Hope* and *Charity*. Can you see them? Now look for the six virtues that are sitting at either side of the Commune. There are the four cardinal virtues that are holding symbolic objects: a sword and crown for *Justice*, an hourglass for *Temperance*, a club and shield for *Fortitude* (Courage) and a mirror for *Prudence*. The other two virtues are *Peace*, dressed in white and lying gently over a heap of weapons with an olive branch in her hand, and *Magnanimity* who is dispensing crowns and coins.

Have you been able to find all these elements? Can you try to apply the various elements of the fresco to a community/leadership context with which you are familiar?

Character Justice

We have just seen justice as a communal affair, but it is also an important individual virtue that you need to cultivate in your character.

Character justice is an actioned desire that what is due should be given to each, in order to favour the ideal interaction between individuals in a community.

Let's unpack this definition with some personal questions.

- Do you experience justice as a desire that is transformed into action? Is justice something that you feel and want? Does it then lead you to concrete action? Do you, for example, feel a desire to see more financial equality? And does this lead you to make generous contributions to the welfare of those that are less well off than you?
- Do you feel a desire that what is due should be given to your neighbour? Do you tend to see the rights of all individuals and recognize what is "due" to them? Do you feel desires for greater

economic equity, for more freedom of speech, for human dignity, for fair wages, or even just to see an elderly person have a seat in a crowded bus?

- Do you seek to favour ideal interaction between individuals in a community? Do you suffer in seeing communities devastated by injustice? Do you engage in concrete actions to establish and maintain justice in the communities to which you belong?

Justice is also expressed in the related virtues of *equity*, *fairness*, *honesty* and in *obedience to the laws* of men and of God. It is seen when you *respect* everyone's rights and treat your neighbour for the common good without distinction of rank or position. *Severity* should be included as a related virtue because there is a time to be inflexible in the administering punishment when right reason requires it. *Concord* is also connected to justice as the effort to establish harmonious human relations.

Does this describe you? If so, well done, you are a just person.

The Opposing Vices

Stanley Hauerwas suggests that, by nature, we either acquire habits of justice or of injustice. Growing up an American Southerner, he tells of how he grew up in a context of discrimination towards African Americans and that it did not occur to him that these arrangements were unjust until he was challenged in his way of seeing things.[41]

This is an important point, for you may well harbour vices of injustice without being aware of them and it is only through training and conscious re-evaluation that you will see the world as it really is. You may, for example, be part of the population of the world that is rich and powerful and that oppress the powerless. Or you may belong to an ethnic group that prevails over another. Or you might be in a Christian leadership position that is designed for power and personal gain. These instances of injustice need to be named and contrasted.

Some of the vices that oppose justice are *illegality*, which breaks rightful laws; *unfairness*, which denies to each what is due; *dishonesty*, which breaks covenants of truthfulness; *partiality*, which accords undue favours; *corruption*, which bends what is right for personal gain and *submissiveness* which passively consents to oppression.

Excess in the virtue of justice is found in oppressive *tyranny* and in merciless law enforcement, which is why the virtue of *mercy* always needs to be in dialogue with justice to mitigate its harshness. An excess in justice can also led us to be *unduly judgemental* of others and to being *legalistic* in criticising imperfections on the grounds of unrealistic expectations.

Do any of these describe you? If they do, and if your score in the Virtue Test was low in this virtue, then you may want to work on the virtue of justice in your character.

A Story of Justice

In *The Brothers Karamazov*, Dostoevsky moves our spirit around issues of justice with the following dialogue between Ivan and Alyosha.

> "There was in those days a general of aristocratic connections, the owner of great estates, one of those men – somewhat exceptional, I believe, even then – who, retiring from the service into a life of leisure, are convinced that they've earned absolute power over the lives of their subjects. There were such men then. So our general, settled on his property of two thousand souls, lives in pomp, and domineers over his poor neighbours as though they were dependents and buffoons. He has kennels of hundreds of hounds and nearly a hundred dog-boys – all mounted, and in uniform.
>
> "One day a serf-boy, a little child of eight, threw a stone in play and hurt the paw of the general's favourite hound. 'Why is my favourite dog lame?' He is told that the boy threw a stone that hurt the dog's paw. 'So you did it.' The general looked the child up and down. 'Take him.' He was taken – taken from his mother and kept shut up all night. Early that morning the general comes out on horseback, with the hounds, his dependents, dog-boys, and huntsmen, all mounted around him in full hunting parade. The servants are summoned for their edification, and in front of them all stands the mother of the child. The child is brought from the lock-up. It's a gloomy, cold, foggy, autumn day, a capital day for hunting. The general orders the child to be undressed; the child is stripped naked. He shivers, numb with terror, not daring to cry . . . 'Make him run,' commands the general. 'Run! run!' shout the dog-boys. The boy runs . . . 'At him!' yells the general, and he sets the

whole pack of hounds on the child. The hounds catch him, and tear him to pieces before his mother's eyes! . . . I believe the general was afterwards declared incapable of administering his estates."

"Well – what did he deserve? To be shot? To be shot for the satisfaction of our moral feelings? Speak, Alyosha!"

"To be shot," murmured Alyosha, lifting his eyes to Ivan with a pale, twisted smile. . . . Ivan for a minute was silent, his face became all at once very sad.

"Listen! I took the case of children only to make my case clearer. Of the other tears of humanity with which the earth is soaked from its crust to its centre, I will say nothing . . . I must have justice, or I will destroy myself. And not justice in some remote infinite time and space, but here on earth, and that I could see myself. I have believed in it. I want to see it, and if I am dead by then, let me rise again, for if it all happens without me, it will be too unfair."

Later in the text, Ivan states: "I don't want the mother to embrace the oppressor who threw her son to the dogs! She dare not forgive him!"[42]

What feelings are roused in you as you read this story?

✅ Verify

Before proceeding, verify your basic understanding of the virtue of justice.[43]

(a) The four "cardinal" virtues are prudence, justice, temperance and courage.

❑ True
❑ False

(b) There are two domains of the virtue of justice: _____ and

_____ .

(c) In the *Allegory of Good Government* Justice is directly connected to the virtues of

_____ and _____ .

(d) Fill in the missing words: Justice is an actioned _____ that

what is _____ should be given in order to favour the ideal

_____ between individuals in a _____ .

(e) Write a "sister virtue" of justice (even in your own language).

_____

(f) Write one vice that opposes justice (even in your own language).

_____

(g) In the dialogue between the Karamazov brothers, what Christian attitude is apparently in

tension with justice? _____

Act: Engage Your Character Friend

This week you will need to meet with your character friend for a third time. Write the time/date of your meeting in the box below:

> [ ]

If you are working with a group, a meeting with your Character Friend Triplet will be part of your weekly group meeting, so you do not need to plan it separately.

Here is a suggested outline for your time together:

1. Give account of your habituation plan.

2. Talk about communal justice as you have considered it this week. Analyse the fresco on the *Allegory of Good Government* and discuss where you can see analogies or shortfalls in your own country and/or community.

3. Talk about individual justice as a virtue and ask your friend for critical input around this virtue in your life. Read the story by Dostoevsky and discuss the feelings that are aroused by it. Discuss the issue of justice and forgiveness, commenting on what Ivan states: "I don't want the mother to embrace the oppressor who threw her son to the dogs! She dare not forgive him!" How do you, as a Christian, respond to a call like this to "not forgive" but rather to punish. Is forgiveness and letting the guilty go unpunished always the only possible Christian response?

Write a few brief notes in the box below of how your meeting went.

> [ ]

Bible Study: Justice and John the Baptist

Read: Luke 3:1–20

This week you have learnt more about the virtue of justice. Now you will engage in a brief Bible study about justice from the preaching of John the Baptist.

John the Baptist is well known as the prophet who prepared the way for the coming of Jesus the Messiah. He did so by calling to repentance. But what was the emphasis of John the Baptist's preaching? What was it that needed repentance? As we look at the text in Luke 3, we see that the core of John's message is related to justice.

We have defined justice as "giving each his due" and in the quotation of Isaiah, we find the metaphors of "making paths straight," "filling in valleys," "lowering mountains," "smoothing out rough ways." So, in a world of crooked paths, differences that need redressing and areas of roughness, correction is needed through justice.

This becomes clear in John's demands on the would-be followers of Jesus:

- if you have two shirts, share one (vs. 11)
- if you have more food than others, share it with the hungry (vs. 11)
- if you collect taxes, just ask for what is fair (vs. 13)
- if you have power, do not use it to extort favours or accuse others to your advantage (vs. 14)
- if are an employee, don't demand more pay than what is due to you (vs. 14)
- if you are not rightfully related to a woman, don't engage in an intimate relationship with her (vs. 19).

These are all instances of paths that need to be made straight. Of dues that need to be rightly given. Of justice that needs to be part of our character as disciples of Jesus. In the face of unjust interactions between individuals and the community, John makes an appeal to repent.

And we see that John practices what he preaches when it comes to baptizing Jesus. Here, he gives what is rightfully due, not abusing of his position of popularity and influence, but recognizing that he is not worthy to even untie Jesus's sandals.

Now respond: Sometimes we say that, to "come to Jesus" you need to do nothing. And of course, salvation is by faith alone. But the story of John the Baptist shows us that something *does* need to be done. Preparation is needed.

And this preparation involves repentance that may specifically have to do with justice.

When you share the gospel, do you invite to repentance? Do you ever specifically address issues of justice with a would-be follower of Jesus? Write a few sentences in the box below to describe your experience and to reflect on where you might need to reconsider your evangelistic approaches.

🙏 A Prayer

Lord, grant me the courage of John the Baptist to speak out against injustice. And with that, change my own character to be more just and accept my commitment to shape my actions according to justice.

This week you have built your virtue literacy by focusing on the virtue of justice. Next week you will look at the virtue of compassion.

Date completed: _____

Week 18

Being Compassionate

See this outward-looking, social virtue in your life

To build your virtue literacy further, this week you will focus on the virtue of compassion. Before you engage with the content for this week, take a moment for a habituation check.

Habituation Check 8. This is the eighth week of practicing your habituation plan, journal below to monitor your practice.

	Journal entry:
❑ I applied my habituation plan well this week ❑ I only marginally applied my habituation plan ❑ I forgot/was too busy to apply my habituation plan	

Being in Someone Else's Shoes

The virtue of *compassion* can be considered a social virtue because it has to do with the way that you interact with others around you, and in particular with those who are suffering and in need.

Compassion is the ability to stand with others in their distress and to take the reality of your neighbour seriously. It is an active disposition towards sharing and supporting those who are facing adverse circumstances. The roots of the Latin word *compassio* literally mean to "suffer with."

Simply put, compassion is a character trait whereby you put yourself in someone else's shoes, listening to them, sympathizing with their needs and responding with works of mercy. By nature, we tend to see our own perspectives and feel our own needs. When you develop the virtue of compassion, you take on another's perspective and feel their needs. Some have suggested that compassion is the virtue that erases the distinction between yourself and others. In this way, compassion is foundational to other social virtues, including *justice*, *kindness*, *honesty* and *love*, for it helps you become aware of those around you.

Is compassion important? Yes. In the words of the Dalai Lama: "Love and compassion are necessities, not luxuries. Without them, humanity cannot survive."[44]

Works of Mercy

The virtue of compassion is complemented by the virtue of *mercy* which acts in concrete ways to relieve suffering. A simplified distinction is that whereas compassion is a feeling of empathy, mercy is a choice of action. In the Christian tradition we therefore speak of "works of mercy" as concrete expressions of compassion.

But what are these works of mercy? Fourteen of them have been identified, the first seven are "corporal" because they deal with physical needs, and the other seven are "spiritual" because they relieve spiritual suffering.

In relation to the corporal works of mercy, there is a notable story that takes place at the beginning of the seventeenth century in Naples (Italy). Seven young noblemen began to meet in a hospital to provide food for those afflicted by incurable diseases. In time, their work became the *Pio Monte della Misericordia*, an organization that collected vast amounts of money and coordinated a large organization that was devoted to works of mercy. The organization explicitly engaged in each of the "seven works of mercy," consisting in:

1. feeding the hungry
2. giving drink to the thirsty
3. sheltering the homeless
4. visiting the sick

5. visiting the prisoners

6. burying the dead

7. and giving alms to the poor

Many other organizations around the world have taken the words of Jesus in Matthew 25 literally and have brought immense relief and care to those in suffering and need.

But mercy does not only deal with physical needs. When it comes to spiritual needs, seven spiritual works of mercy have been identified to bring relief from spiritual suffering. They are:

1. admonishing the sinner

2. instructing the ignorant

3. counselling the doubtful

4. bearing wrongs patiently

5. forgiving offenses willingly

6. comforting the afflicted

7. and praying for those in need

Is the Virtue of Compassion in Your Character?

Here are some questions to ask yourself concerning the virtue of compassion.

1. To what extent do you notice and attend to situations that require compassion?

2. How often do you bend your will to act in ways that provide relief to those around you? Can you think of recent instances where you have brought aid and relief to someone?

3. Are you familiar with feelings of empathy? Do you feel the predicaments and suffer for the pain of others?

4. Do you want to be less egocentric and more altruistic? Is it your ambition to make a difference in the suffering of the world?

5. How do others perceive you? Would those that know you describe you as someone who puts themselves in someone else's shoes?

The practice of works of mercy has many possible expressions today. Take a pencil and put a check mark besides any of the following that you are involved in:

- I see to the proper nutrition of my loved ones
- I support agencies that feed the hungry
- I educate myself about world hunger
- I avoid wasting food
- I help my neighbours in need
- I provide support in the wake of natural disasters
- I donate clothes in good conditions to agencies that provide assistance to the poor
- I spend quality time with those who are sick
- I do volunteer work in a hospital
- I am a primary caregiver for a sick relative
- I support and/or participate in ministries to the incarcerated
- I support agencies that advocate for those that are unjustly imprisoned
- I pray for the families of inmates
- I give to mendicants who ask for help
- I make donations to charities that help the poor
- I support or volunteer in a hospice
- I spend time with widows and widowers
- I offer sympathy to those who are grieving
- I try to learn about the Christian faith so I can share with others
- I share my insights and knowledge with others
- I read good books and encourage others to do the same
- I encourage fellow Christians to remain faithful
- I encourage friends to do what is right
- I respond negatively to prejudice and gossip and walk away from it
- I work at being optimistic
- I try to speak words of hope
- I walk with others through their pain, offering hospitality to suffering without immediately trying to fix things
- I pray for those that have wronged me
- I am ready to forgive those that ask forgiveness of me
- I try to let go of grudges
- I work at not being critical of others

- I give people the benefit of the doubt
- I pray for my friends, family and church
- I pray for those that are in need, even if I do not know them

Surely, you should not expect to check all the boxes, for it is impossible for one person to be actively involved in all the works of mercy at the same time. But if you have checked very few boxes, you may want to evaluate your own character in terms of the virtue of mercy and compassion.

Note: are you able to match the actions in the list with the fourteen works of mercy?

The Opposing Vices

It is easy to see the deficiency of compassion in the vice of *disregard* that has no consideration for the interests or needs of others, in the vice of *selfishness* which always puts yourself in the first place, in the vice of *indifference* where no amount of suffering in others elicits a response and in the vice of *cynicism* where you doubt whether others have genuine needs at all.

Perhaps the excesses of compassion are less obvious, but they need to be carefully understood as they can lead to the vice of *self-annulment*. Benevolence to others must be, in fact, balanced with healthy benevolence to yourself.

Do any of these describe you? If they do, and if your score in the Virtue Test was low in this virtue, then you may want to work further on the virtue of compassion in your character.

Stories of Compassion

Maria Teresa of Calcutta is no doubt one of the most famous women of our time. And what has made her famous is her example of compassion and mercy as she devoted her life to assisting the poorest of the poor in India.

Here is a story told by one of the sisters working with her in the Calcutta slums.

> On my first day with Mother Teresa I went with her to the slums of Motijhil. We would walk the streets and pray. Mother Teresa had a bag with something inside, and she gave me one as well. Inside there was a piece of soap, a towel, a pair of scissors and some vitamins. When we arrived, the children surrounded Mother

Teresa, singing and greeting her. I immediately noticed how dirty they were. Some were very young, while others were older and were holding their younger siblings.

Mother Teresa took me by the hand and led me toward the children to wash them: their noses, hands and feet. And then to fix their hair. She said that this was a fantastic opportunity of serving Jesus.

Despite my love for Jesus, and despite the fact that I really wanted to be like Mother Teresa in her work with the poor and outcast, I found it very challenging to actually reach out and touch the filth that was on these children. But Mother Teresa gave me the key to overcome my hesitation by telling me that each one of these children was Jesus, who waits to be touched by us with love, humility and gratitude. I've never forgotten that lesson of faith in practice.[45]

Maria Teresa of Calcutta offers a second lesson that challenges the notion that compassion is a virtue that is exercised only by those that are more fortunate. In actual fact, it is often the less fortunate that represent the greatest examples of compassion. Maria Teresa tells the following story:

One night a man came to our house and told me: "There is a family with eight children. They haven't eaten for days." I grabbed some food and set off. When I came to them, I saw the faces of those little ones marked by hunger. Their faces showed no pain or sadness, only the profound suffering caused by fasting. I gave the rice to the mother, who divided it into two parts and walked out of the house with half the ration. When she returned, I asked her: "Where did you go?" She gave me a very simple answer: "I went to my neighbours of course. They're hungry too!"

This selflessness didn't surprise me: the poor are really very generous . . . Usually when we suffer, we are so focused on ourselves that we have no time for others.[46]

Verify

Take a few moments to verify your basic understanding of the virtue of compassion.[47]

(a) You are now in your eighth week of habituation. You have met three times with your character friend(s) and are engaging with a fifth virtue as you build your virtue literacy.
❏ True
❏ False

(b) The virtue of compassion means to "suffer with."
❏ True
❏ False

(c) The virtue of mercy has to do with concrete actions to relieve suffering.
❏ True
❏ False

(d) List at least three corporal works of mercy: _____, _____, _____.

(e) List at least three spiritual works of mercy: _____, _____, _____.

(f) Indicate the opposing vice to compassion which is most problematic for you:

_____.

Act: Compassion to Your Parents

In times of increasing selfishness, egoism and individualism, it can be helpful to think of people close to you who need your compassion and mercy. The fifth commandment calls us to "honour our father and mother" and in the context this includes provision for their needs. Compassion towards our parents is a universal value and it should be a priority in our walk as disciples. The Confucian scholar Mencius claimed that the core of mercy is found in serving one's own parents.

Take a moment now to reflect on your stance towards your own parents. Do you have compassion for their needs or are you still a child who demands that they serve you? Is your attitude towards your parents one of helping or of receiving?

Think of a need your parents may have and do something for them this week. Write down your chosen act of mercy toward your parents in the box below.

If your parents are not alive or not available to you, choose another significant elderly person in your life to whom you might exercise an act of mercy.

Bible Study: Works of Mercy and Judgement

Read: Matthew 25:31–45

The corporal works of mercy that we have seen in this lesson are found in Matthew 25.

In the context, Jesus is teaching about being accountable and about preparing for judgement. Chapter 25 contains the parable of the ten virgins waiting to meet the bridegroom, followed by the parable of the master and his stewards and concluding with the metaphor of the sheep and the goats.

Each one of these images comes with a warning. The virgins are to "watch" (25:13). The stewards are to "gain more" (25:20, 22), and we should aim to "be sheep rather than goats" (25:33). But what does this mean in practice?

Jesus makes a practical application of these images by prescribing a specific list of works of mercy that we should be engaged in as we prepare to meet him. This is the list of seven corporal works of mercy that you have seen above:

- feed the hungry
- give drink to the thirsty
- offer hospitality to strangers
- clothe those needing clothes
- look after the sick
- visit the prisoners

The text is dramatically sharp in indicating both positive reward and negative punishment in relation to these works. When we perform these works of mercy towards someone, we will be welcomed to the wedding room, we will receive a "well done" from the master, we will be good sheep and it will be as if we were serving Jesus himself. If we do not engage in these works of mercy, we will be separated out as the unprepared virgins, treated as poor stewards and considered as goats that will come under judgement.

Now respond: Matthew 25 is a text that speaks to the heart of your walk as a disciple. There are many important aspects of discipleship, including your spirituality, your leadership qualities and your commitment to share the gospel. But you cannot afford to leave out the works of mercy.

In the box below, write down at least one work of mercy that you commit to performing in the coming months. Perhaps this could be an additional habituation task to add to what you are already committed to.

 A Prayer

Lord guard my heart from disregard, selfishness, indifference and cynicism. Show me the works of mercy that you would have me do and grant me the virtue of compassion to perform them.

> This week you have built your virtue literacy by focusing on the virtue of compassion. Next week you will look at the virtue of diligence.

Date completed: _____

Week 19

Being Diligent

See this civic virtue in your life

As you continue your habituation plan, this week you will think about the virtue of diligence.

Habituation Check 9. This is the ninth week of practicing your habituation plan, journal below to monitor your practice.

	Journal entry:
❑ I applied my habituation plan well this week	
❑ I only marginally applied my habituation plan	
❑ I forgot/was too busy to apply my habituation plan	

A Virtue for Work

Life is work. Sometimes paid work, sometimes unpaid work. Sometimes the menial work of duties, sometimes the inspired work of genius. Sometimes the work of creation and sometimes the work of recreation.

Within such a broad definition, consider the following as examples of work:

- laying bricks to build a house
- designing software

- going shopping and cooking
- preparing carefully for our summer vacations
- making our bed and tidying up our room
- doing our homework
- compiling footnotes for an academic thesis
- completing a piece of pottery
- writing poetry or composing music
- training carefully for sporting competitions
- and so on . . .

If in your mind the word "work" is associated only with weary duties or with paid employment, you should reconsider. You may have heard friends say that they do not want to "live to work," but that they want to "work to live." You may even believe that yourself. But think again. Is work only something evil that must be endured, or can it be a deep source of joy and satisfaction?

A long time ago, Aristotle suggested that life's greatest joys are not what we do *apart* from the work of our life, but what we do *with* the work of our life.

What then are the virtues that accompany us as we work? Actually almost all of the virtues can be applied to work: *courage, temperance, patience, justice, humility* and so forth. But the one virtue that stands out for its relevance to work is the virtue of *diligence*.

Is the Virtue of Diligence in Your Character?

Let us begin with a definition: "Diligence is ongoing zealous attention to your actions and work." Notice a few things about this definition:

- Diligence is ongoing – it is something that lasts over time and includes the virtue of constancy.
- Diligence is zealous – it entails working with a passion to do well and includes the virtue of *ambition* that finds legitimate pride in achievement.
- Diligence needs attention – in diligence there is a care of detail which includes the virtue of *attentiveness*, together with an *awareness* of where improvement is needed and a creative commitment to *excellence*.
- Diligence relates to all your actions, whether at home, school or in the office, at work or at play, alone or in community.

If you are a diligent person, you exhibit a work ethic, meaning you have a moral commitment to doing what needs to be done and to doing it well, even when no one is looking and even when you are not being paid for what you do. This might also be called the virtue of *duty* that helps you cultivate good work habits.

Diligence can be seen in very practical virtues like *punctuality*, where you are on time, where you do things within the right time frame and where you make a wise use of your time. But diligence is also seen in the virtue of *orderliness* that contrasts the natural chaos and disorder of life by working at keeping things in a place of beauty and order.

Together with diligence, we can think about *decency* as living in conformity to right standards of *purity, cleanliness* and *dignity*. Decency includes the ordering of one's person, things, speech, sexuality and a right relationship with food and other substances.

Does this describe you? If so, well done, you are a diligent person.

The Opposing Vices

The deficiency vices of diligence can easily be seen in *laziness, sloth* and *acedia*. Relative to these, the Bible has much to say. Proverbs 6:6 tells the lazy man to learn from the ants, and 2 Thessalonians 3:6 condemns those that are idle, urging them to "earn the food they eat."

The excesses of diligence are not that easy to spot. Increasingly however, we see *obsessive compulsive* behaviours and *overly controlling* attitudes that evidence misdirected diligence. Also, there are *workaholics* that have fallen off the deep end of diligence, where work has become the only end in life, at the cost of everything else. These vices drain vitality and need to be mitigated by the practices of *recreation* and by habits of resting well and enjoying the goodness of life.

Spiritualization is a particular vice related to work that can afflict Christians. Spirituality is good, and as such it might be considered a virtue. But too much spirituality can turn into vice, and nowhere is this clearer than in relation to work. It is easy, in fact, to make the mistake of separating your life into what you consider as "spiritual" and what you consider as "material." So you may think that going to church, evangelizing or praying are "spiritual" things, in contrast with going to work, making your bed or studying for a secular degree that are "material" things.

But this is an unhealthy separation that creates a false hierarchy between what is worthy of discipleship and what is not. As a disciple of Jesus, you should consider your work as an essential part of who you are and of what it means to follow him. God himself worked and called his work good. And he has given you the gift of working diligently as part of your call to follow him.

Bezalel is a wonderful example of this holistic vision of life and work. He was fundamentally an artisan, but the Bible says that he was chosen and "filled with the Spirit of God, with wisdom, with understanding, with knowledge and with all kinds of skills to make artistic designs" (Exod 35:30, 32). His work was a gift from and to God.

If you are lacking in diligence, and if your score in the Virtue Test was low in this virtue, then you might need to work on this in your character.

A Story of Diligence

The *Choice of Hercules* is an ancient story told by Socrates that has inspired artists throughout history. As you read the story, view the painting of Annibale Carracci *Hercules at the Crossroads* by using the QR code below.

(Hercules at the Crossroads – Wikipedia)[48]

The story goes as follows.[49]

Long before he became a Greek hero, young Hercules found himself at a fork in the road, where he stopped to contemplate his future and what course of life he should pursue. Uncertain about which path to take in life, he was approached by two goddesses, each coming from a different direction.

One of the goddesses rushed in to ensure she met Hercules first. She craved attention and was dressed to seduce him. Although she told Hercules that her friends called her Happiness, her real name was Vice. She promised Hercules that if he followed her down her path, he would have a life filled with pleasure beyond most men's wildest dreams. It would be an easy life without hardships or struggle. A shortcut to Happiness, as she put it. All Hercules had to do was follow her and he would forever be out of the reach of pain and misery.

The other goddess listened and then approached Hercules. She was humble and plainly dressed, though naturally beautiful. When asked her name, she answered some call me Labour, but others know me as Virtue.

To Hercules's surprise, she told him, "I have nothing to promise you, young Hercules, except what you will earn through your strength." She told him that if he followed her pathway, he would have to face many hardships, perhaps more than most men could handle, and that he would have to suffer and endure significant losses along the way.

However, she told him that her path would allow him to prove himself to the gods, earn true happiness and eternal fame by reflecting on his own praiseworthy and noble deeds. She ended by telling Hercules that a life of easy comforts and pleasure is merely an illusion.

After listening to both women, Hercules looked at Virtue and said, "I will take you as my guide! The road of Labour and honest effort shall be mine." With that, he put his hand into that of Virtue and entered the path of growth.

Verify

Verify your understanding of the place of work in Christian discipleship and the virtue of diligence.[50]

(a) Work is an evil that must be endured.   ❏ True
  ❏ False

(b) We should be careful in creating hierarchies between dimensions of discipleship that are

_____ and _____.

(c) Diligence is ongoing zealous attention to your actions and work.   ❏ True
  ❏ False

(d) Other virtues that are associated with diligence are (name two):

_____ and _____.

(e) Vices that oppose diligence are (name two):

_____ and _____.

(f) A vice-by-excess of humility is _____.

 Act: What Is Your Work?

Use the space below to list ten elements that make up your life of "work." Make this list as broad and creative as possible.

Now look at each element in your list and ask yourself: what does diligence look like in this area of work? Also list possible areas of improvement in each element of your work.

📖 Bible Study: Work in the Bible

Read: Ephesians 6:5–8

The Bible has a lot to say about work and diligence. Here is a list of statements from the Bible about work. Match these statements with the verses under the table.[51]

1) We should be diligent in paying other workers what is right.   _____

2) We should contribute to the costs of life through work in   _____
order to live in an orderly way.

3) We should not be lazy at work.   _____

4) We should not work only when the "boss" is watching.   _____

5) Work in the fallen condition can be frustrating.   _____

6) Work is a gift of God to mankind.   _____

7) Work is good.   _____

Focus now on Ephesians 6:5–8 that features two key principles to regulate your diligent commitment to work. Although the direct context relates to slaves and masters, the principles can apply equally to you.

Principle 1: All work has value for God (Ephesians 6:8). The text says that "the Lord will reward each one," regardless of their working condition. The Lord rewards for (secular) work because it is valuable for him. For the slaves reading this epistle, this meant that fetching water, cleaning the horse stalls, washing tunics and making bread had value in the eyes of God.

Principle 2: In our work we must look to God (Ephesians 6:6). The text says that, in your work, you are to "do the will of God from your heart." If you are dissatisfied with the work that you do, you may be seeking for approval from the wrong source. If you work to "win the favour of men," you will often be disappointed and may lose your motivation to do your work diligently. But if you consider yourself as a worker of God, who has asked you to do the work at hand, and appreciates what you do, then your heart will be simpler and undivided ("sincere" in vs 5). This is a great source of strength in doing your work wholeheartedly.

Now respond: Go back to the list above of ten elements that make up your life of "work." Read them out loud and for each of them say, "This has value for God, and I will look to God as I do this work."

So, for example: "Making my bed in the morning has value for God and I will look to God as I make my bed well." Or: "Driving the bus has value for God and I will look to God as I drive as best I can and treat my passengers as God's creatures."

How did it feel to say these words? Once you have completed this exercise, describe your feelings in the box below:

A Prayer

Lord, I commit to be diligent in all my work, of whatever kind, recognizing that it is valuable to you. I look to you for approval, even when I may not receive it from those around me and I ask for a simple heart to find joy in working wholeheartedly.

> This week you have built your virtue literacy by focusing on the virtue of diligence. Next week you will look at the virtue of gratitude.

Date completed: _____

Week 20

Being Grateful

See this personal virtue in your life

This week, as you continue your habituation plan, you will focus on the virtue of gratitude. This week you will also meet again with your character friend.

Habituation Check 10. This is the tenth week of practicing your habituation plan, journal below to monitor your practice.

❑ I applied my habituation plan well this week	Journal entry:
❑ I only marginally applied my habituation plan	
❑ I forgot/was too busy to apply my habituation plan	

Gratitude and Other Virtues

Gratitude is an affirmation of goodness. It is a confirmation that good things and positive gifts and benefits exist in our world and life. Gratitude does not negate the fact that suffering, challenges, burdens, and pain also exist. But it allows us to take a step back and see the bigger picture in which we also find goodness.

The Roman philosopher Cicero claimed that *gratitude* is not only the greatest virtue of all but also the virtue which is the parent of all the other virtues.

> What is moral gratitude, if not dear sentiment towards our parents? Who are gentlemen and countrymen, if not those that recall the benefits received from the mother land? Who are the virtuous, devoted to the gods, if not those who deserve their grace? What pleasure can there be in life without friendship? And what friendship can there be without gratitude? Who of us, with a noble education, does not bear fond memory of those who educated our souls? Most surely, it is fitting for man not only to be bound to the benefits he has received, but to express benevolence and approval of their source.[52]

This relationship between the virtue of gratitude and other virtues is an important starting point. The virtues are, in fact, connected to each other and no virtue should be studied or cultivated in isolation.

Gratitude has sometimes been placed within an "allocentric quintet" of virtues. This is a set of five virtues that focus our attention on others (the word *allos*, in fact, means "others" and is in contrast with *ego*-centric). The five virtues that put others at the centre of our attention are *forgiveness, humility, generosity, gratitude* and *compassion*. These virtues stand on their own, but they also feed and strengthen each other. So, for example, the virtue of forgiveness is stronger if you are generous toward the wrongdoings of others. Likewise, you will find it easier to cultivate the virtue of humility when you benefit from the generosity of those around you.

In particular, you can understand gratitude better when you place it in relationship with the virtues of generosity and compassion (which you engaged with in Week 18). The more you are compassionate, the more you will be sensitive to acts of generosity, and that, in turn, will help you be more grateful. And vice-versa. The more you exercise gratitude, the more you will be compassionate and generous.[53] So if your character is wanting in compassion, it might not come as a surprise that gratitude is also an area of weakness.

The Importance of Being Grateful

Why then is gratitude so important?

Gratitude, first of all, is good for others, and has been shown to reinforce social bonds and foster better communities. Gratitude is considered a core virtue in addressing the challenges of society today. This is not a new consideration. Confucian philosophy considered gratitude as a fundamental virtue to maintain social harmony and good relationships.

Gratitude is also good for you. Studies have demonstrated that those who are grateful enjoy a greater sense of wellbeing, satisfaction with life and better mental health. In his *Letters to Lucilius*, Seneca writes that:

> Gratitude is a good thing for ourselves . . . For if wickedness makes men unhappy and virtue makes men blest, and if it is a virtue to be grateful, then the return which you have made is only the customary thing, but the thing to which you have attained is priceless.[54]

Gratitude is also an essential element of faith and discipleship. St. Augustine, for example, considered gratitude as the appropriate Christian response to the love and grace of God, especially as he considered the gifts of life and eternal life.

It is not accidental that the term "eucharist," that describes the core Christian liturgical practice, derives from the Greek term "giving thanks." At the core of our walk of faith we find a posture of gratitude. A similar emphasis on gratitude to the divine can be found in other religions as well. In Islam, for example, the practice of daily prayer encourages believers to express gratitude to Allah five times a day for his goodness, and the pillar of fasting is meant to position the believer in a state of gratitude.

Is the Virtue of Gratitude in Your Character?

So what about your own character? Are you a grateful person? Take a few moments to ask yourself the following probing questions:

- Do I see myself as a recipient of gifts from sources beyond myself?
- Do I spend more time complaining about what I don't have than being grateful for what I do have?

- Do I remember favours received or do I take them for granted?
- How often do I say thank you?
- Do I have a demanding spirit of always wanting more from those around me?
- Do I have feelings of deep respect towards those that have helped, guided and cared for me?
- Do others consider me an appreciative person?

Gratitude can be expressed in your character at different levels of maturity. At a basic level you may be grateful for benefits and material items that are self-oriented (e.g. you are thankful for your parents who pay for your university). At higher levels you discover gratitude for benefits that are beyond your immediate personal gain, such as gratitude for the inspirational behaviour of other people (e.g. you are thankful for fire-fighters who risk their lives to save others). This mature level of gratitude often involves gratitude for people and relationships.

The Opposing Vices

Some of the evident vices-by-defect that oppose gratitude are *un-thankfulness*, a *demanding spirit* and *complaining*. These are the vices of those that never say thank you, that always want more and that always posture as a victim.

To have the virtue of gratitude is to be disposed not just to be grateful, but to be grateful in the right ways, to the right people, for the right motivations.[55] This entails that the virtue of gratitude can go wrong in at least three ways.

The virtue of gratitude can go wrong when it is not expressed in the right way. For example, if you go overboard in a profusion of thanks toward a superior, this might be a display of exaggerated politeness or an effort to please, with no underlying sense of true gratitude. This is a vice-by-excess that distorts true gratitude.

The virtue of gratitude can go wrong when it is not expressed to the right people. So it is wrong not to express gratitude towards your parents. But it is also wrong to express gratitude towards those who do not deserve it and who may have treated you wrongly (in this case the virtue of justice or forgiveness may be more appropriate).

Finally, the virtue of gratitude can go wrong when it is not expressed for the right motivation. So gratitude that is associated with sheer obligation, indebtedness or guilt is not genuine gratitude.

A Story of Gratitude

Marcus Aurelius's book *Meditations* begins with a beautiful "letter of gratitude" which amounts to a long list of all the people who have loved him, inspired him and shaped him. He expresses his gratitude in this way because he believes that if we do not celebrate those who have contributed to whom we have become, there will be little left of what we are.

In Marcus Aurelius's list, the longest and most moving expression of gratitude goes to his father. The quotation is a little longer than usual, but it is well worth it.

> I learned from my father gentleness and undeviating constancy in judgments formed after due reflection; not to be puffed up with glory as men understand it; to be laborious and assiduous.
>
> He taught me to give ready hearing to any man who offered anything tending to the common good; to mete out impartial justice to every one; to apprehend rightly when severity and when clemency should be used; to abstain from all impure lusts; and to use humanity towards all men. Thus he left his friends at liberty to sup with him or not, to go abroad with him or not, exactly as they inclined; and they found him still the same if some urgent business had prevented them from obeying his commands.
>
> I learned of him accuracy and patience in council, for he never quitted an enquiry satisfied with first impressions. I observed his zeal to retain his friends without being fickle or over fond; his contentment in every condition; his cheerfulness; his forethought about very distant events; his unostentatious attention to the smallest details; his restraint of all popular applause and flattery . . .
>
> As to the things which make the ease of life, and which fortune can supply in such abundance, he used them without pride, and yet with all freedom: enjoyed them without affectation when they were present, and when absent he found no want of them . . .
>
> His manners were easy, his conversation delightful, but not cloying. He took regular but moderate care of his body, neither as one over fond of life or of the adornment of his person, nor as one who despised these things. Thus, through his own care, he seldom needed any medicines, whether salves or potions. It was his special merit to yield without envy to any who had acquired

any special faculty, as either eloquence, or learning in the Law, in ancient customs, or the like; and he aided such men strenuously, so that every one of them might be regarded and esteemed for his special excellence.

He observed carefully the ancient customs of his forefathers, and preserved, without appearance of affectation, the ways of his native land. He was not fickle and capricious, and loved not change of place or employment. After his violent fits of headache he would return fresh and vigorous to his wonted affairs. Of secrets he had few, and these seldom, and such only as concerned public matters. He displayed discretion and moderation in exhibiting shows for the entertainment of the people, in his public works, in largess and the like; and in all those things he acted like one who regarded only what was right and becoming in the things themselves, and not the reputation that might follow after.

He never bathed at unseasonable hours, had no vanity in building, was never solicitous either about his food or about the make or colour of his clothes, or about the beauty of his servants . . .

He was far from being inhuman, or implacable, or violent; never doing anything with such keenness that one could say he was sweating about it, in all things he reasoned distinctly, as one at leisure, calmly, regularly, resolutely, and consistently . . . To be strong in abstinence and temperate in enjoyment, to be sober in both – these are qualities of a man of perfect and invincible soul.[56]

In an age in which we have learned to be critical of our parents and to think of them frequently in terms of their shortfalls, this expression of praise and gratitude of their virtues (even if imperfect) is revolutionary. If you were asked to write an expression of gratitude to your father, what would you write?

✅ Verify

Verify your understanding of the virtue of gratitude.[57]

(a) Gratitude is an affirmation of goodness.

❏ True
❏ False

(b) Name the virtues in the "allocentric quintet": _____ ,

_____ , _____ ,

_____ .

(c) Gratitude is good for _____ and for _____ .

(d) The core Christian liturgical practice that means "giving thanks" is

_____ .

(e) A mature level of gratitude focuses on people and relationships.

❏ True
❏ False

(f) Name one opposing vice to gratitude: _____ .

Act: Engage Your Character Friend

This week you will meet with your friend for a fourth time. Write the time/
date of your meeting in the box below:

> [empty box]

If you are working with a group, a meeting with your Character Friend Triplet
will be part of your weekly group meeting, so you do not need to plan it
separately.

Here is a suggested outline for your time together:

1. Give account of your habituation plan.

2. Talk about the virtue of gratitude that you have considered this week.
   Read together out loud the words of Marcus Aurelius to his father
   and share with each other why you are grateful for your own fathers
   (imperfect as they might be). Then share why you are grateful for
   each other as friends.

3. Ask your character friend for feedback on gratefulness in your own
   character. How would they rank you? Where might they see areas
   of improvement?

Write a few brief notes in the box below of how your meeting went.

> [empty box]

📖 Bible Study: Nine Ungrateful Lepers

Read: Luke 17:11–19

Perhaps no one story in the Bible speaks more clearly about gratitude than the story of Jesus healing the ten lepers.

You may know the story. As Jesus is on his way to Jerusalem, he is met by ten lepers who cry out to be healed. Jesus tells them to go to the priest and, as they go, they are all cleansed. At that point, only one of the nine comes back to say thank you.

Here are some observations on how the virtues of gratitude, compassion, humility and generosity are woven together in this story.

1. It is those that need help who take the initiative. They ask for help. Their request is specific and urgent. And in them we see the virtue of humility.

2. The act of generosity from Jesus is genuine, and matches their deepest needs, both physical and relational.

3. These men really needed help. Leprosy was a terrible disease. Mortal, disfiguring and alienating. We see in Jesus the virtue of compassion, which is what sparks gratitude in the tenth leper.

4. Those that ask for help believe that Jesus can do something for them. They call him Master and have come to him because there is an element of faith.

5. Jesus could have ignored them. He had no obligation towards them and could have safely told them to go away, as that was the acceptable social norm. But Jesus is generous and goes above and beyond the call of duty.

The story has two conclusions. In one we see virtue and in the other we see vice.

Vice. Nine lepers are healed and never come back to say thank you. Jesus wonders why . . . Had their suffering hardened them to believe they deserved help? Were they simply too busy as they ran back to their families? Were they (paradoxically) too proud to undergo what they may have perceived as the further humiliation of gratitude? Had they spent lives in which their character had very little to be grateful for, and thus now no gratitude emerged even in the face of the greatest gift?

Virtue. One leper is healed and comes back to say thank you. It is not coincidence that he is a Samaritan. He was the one that deserved less as his people were in enmity with Jews like Jesus. But what we see is unashamed humility as he throws himself at the feet of Jesus saying thank you over and over again.

Now respond: How many times have you been like the nine lepers towards God or toward your neighbour? Do you need to "come back" and say thank you to someone for something? In the box below, write the name of one person that you are going to thank this week for something.

A Prayer

Lord, show me if I am like the nine lepers. If I do not see the good that is done to me because of the suffering I have been through. If I do not take the time to express gratitude. If I take blessings for granted and always demand more. I am at your feet to say thank you, for my life, for the good that comes my way, for the people that love me imperfectly, for my life in you.

> This week you have habituated, met with your character friend(s)
> and built your virtue literacy by focusing on the virtue of
> gratitude. Next week you will look at the virtue of passion.

Date completed: _____

Week 21

Being Passionate

See this personal virtue in your life

This week, as you continue your habituation plan, you will focus on the vice of *acedia* and the countering virtue of *passion*. Before you engage with the content for this week, take a moment for a habituation check.

Habituation Check 11. This is the eleventh week of practicing your habituation plan, journal below to monitor your practice.

❏ I applied my habituation plan well this week

❏ I only marginally applied my habituation plan

❏ I forgot/was too busy to apply my habituation plan

Journal entry:

The Vice of Acedia in Times of Boredom

Rather than start with the virtue of *passion*, this week we begin with the vice to which this virtue remedies: the vice of *acedia*.

Acedia is the fourth of the seven capital vices. These are considered as those which generate everything that is against virtue. One way of understanding the capital vices is as different instances of love gone wrong. The first three capital vices of *pride*, *envy* and *wrath* are instances of love that has gone wrong towards God and neighbour. The last three capital vices of *greed*, *gluttony* and *lust* are instead instances of love gone wrong towards things.

Among the seven, *acedia* stands on its own. For acedia is the lack of love towards anything and anybody. It is worse than love gone wrong or love misdirected: it is love that has gone out. The term acedia, in fact, literally means "no care." It is the state of our soul in which we no longer care for anything or anyone.

The vice of acedia is the least known, the hardest to define, the most controversial to identify and the hardest to face. It can be described as the lack of passion, and is sometimes translated sloth, inertia and apathy. It is a condition where the soul is deflated and where we are generally not interested in anything. It is what the French poet Baudelaire called "ennui" (suggesting that it is the worst of all vices) and what Billie Eilish sings about in her song "Bored": "bored, I'm so bored . . ."

Acedia typically flourishes in the following conditions:

- when you are focused on yourself and self-realization as the most important value
- when you have too much
- when you live in protection and think you deserve entertainment
- when you don't have to work hard or wait to have what you want
- when you've never had to undergo discipline or real hardship
- when your main obsession is to flee from boredom
- when you abide by the law of diminishing returns, and the more you find entertainment the more you are bored
- when enjoying almost immediate fulfilment of most of your desires, you experiment a corresponding fading of interest in everything

Can you see how acedia might be one of the prevailing vices in your own society?

Is Acedia in Your Character?

Read the following statements and tick any of the boxes that are recurring for you. If you've thought (or said) this kind of thing, it may be an indicator of the vice of acedia.

- Everything is heavy.
- I want to get away and let sleep take over, rule out everything.
- My world drifts by slowly, without remarkable emotions.
- I feel I have lost all sense, and have no vitality to offer, no enthusiasm to share and no energy to invest in any dream.
- I feel I am a bored spectator of the world.
- It seems to me that everything is nothing but a rerun of the same show, the same actors, the same scripts . . . why should I bother?
- I live as reflex, and people to me are cogs in the machinery.
- My life is run over by a placid and devastating sense of sameness.

A word of caution may be necessary at this point. Acedia is a controversial vice because the symptoms of laziness, lethargy, indolence, melancholy and sadness can be similar to those caused by psychological conditions like depression. The two should not be confused, and although character education can be of help in psychological states, you should not undermine their complex roots and should seek professional help when needed.

Cultivating the Virtue of Passion

If your character has been sapped by the vice of acedia, you need to work on its countering virtue which is *passion*.

What is the virtue of passion? It is fundamentally the reverse of all that we have described above as acedia. It is strong love for people and a healthy love for things. It includes the virtue of diligence, as a zealous attention to your actions and work. Its synonyms are zeal, pugnacity, attentiveness, work and orderliness. Passion is also marked by *ambition* as a positive virtue that finds legitimate pride in achievement and in desiring excellence in all things.

The virtue of passion is, in short, a will to live and a will to love, accompanied by emotions of hope and constructive actions.

As passion counters acedia, it leads us out of boredom and into a life of flourishing.

A Metaphor of Passion

This week you will look at a metaphor for the virtue of passion. Just like stories, metaphors also have a powerful impact in developing your virtue literacy because they give you mental images of virtue. So here is a mental image for passion that comes from the philosopher Plato.[58]

Plato offers a three-fold image of the human soul:

1. The Man, which is the intellectual part of the soul that is driven by the desire of knowledge.

2. The Lion, that represents the emotive or spirited part that feels anger, shame, courage and excitement and is driven by the desire of honour.

3. The Monster, which instead signifies desire and is driven by cravings for pleasure.

In today's society the Man is being lost, as the desire for knowledge is replaced by the search for competence and the slow pleasure of cultivating knowledge is potentially delegated to artificial intelligence.

The Lion, which best represents passion, also flounders in an environment that lacks motivating projects and grand visions and in which there is no utopia, no higher culture, no ideal state, no model citizenship, no grand aspirations and no universal values. In these conditions the Lion falls asleep or wanders aimlessly with passing flirts of spirit. Continual exposure to immediate gratification, without courtship, waiting, or building up to a climax saps enthusiasm, motivation and curiosity and ends passion.

That leaves us with the Monster, which might well be the prevailing force today. The Monster in each of us represents the search for experiences, individual expression and personal pleasure as the main guiding force. Having silenced the rational Man and narcotized the spirited Lion, the profit-seeking Monster in the soul takes over in shaping contemporary identities and provides fertile ground for acedia.

As a Christian disciple, made in the image of God, it is your call to cultivate all aspects of your being. And cultivating the virtue of passion is a way to revive the Man and the Lion in you.

✓ Verify

Before proceeding, briefly verify your understanding of the vice of acedia and the virtue of passion.[59]

(a) Which three capital vices are "love gone wrong towards God and neighbour"?

_____ , _____ , _____

(b) Which three capital vices are "love gone wrong towards things"?

_____ , _____ , _____

(c) Which capital vice is "the absence of love"? _____

(d) Acedia may be one of the most prevailing vices in your context?

☐ True
☐ False

(e) Acedia and depression are the same thing.

☐ True
☐ False

(f) What is the positive virtue that finds legitimate pride in achievement and that desires excellence? _____

(g) Which of the three images offered by Plato embodies the virtue of passion?

_____

Act: Do something ambitious

One of the debilitating effects of acedia is that it drains your energies and removes desire to do anything. It is like being overweight, where excessive weight contributes to removing your ability to perform physical exercise. But just as the remedy to being overweight is found in exercise, so the remedy to acedia is found in doing things. This requires your will.

The exercise this week is to do something ambitious. It does not need to be anything major or excessively time consuming. The word "ambitious" simply means doing something different to improve something in your life. You could paint the walls of your room, clean out a shelf in your basement, try a new haircut, rent a bicycle and go for a ride in a park where you have never been, or cook a creative recipe for a friend.

In the space below, journal briefly about what you have willed to do, how you have done it, and how you felt afterwards.

 Bible Study: The Sea or the Mountain?

Read: Exodus 14:12 and Luke 1:39

This week you have focused on acedia and passion. In the *Divine Comedy*, Dante quotes two biblical stories to illustrate the vice of acedia and the remedial virtue of passion. One takes place at the sea, the other takes place on a mountain. Here they are.

The sea. The story by the sea contains a negative example of acedia. In it, Dante notes the passiveness of the children of Israel as they have just escaped from Egypt:

- they are standing before the Red Sea
- Pharaoh is coming with all his chariots to get them

- they are petrified with fear
- and in their heart is the sin of acedia, summed up in the sentence "leave us alone."

The memory of the pitiful condition of being slaves and making bricks under the sun is still fresh in their mind, but all they can say is "it would have been better if you had left us alone." They have just seen the phenomenal deeds of God in the ten plagues, but now all they can say is "leave us alone." They were about to witness one of the greatest deeds in their history, the parting of the Red Sea and the defeat of the Egyptian army, but their heart is dead. "Leave us alone."

And here we see acedia: they have no love for themselves; no love for their condition or for their families; no love for God nor anticipation of his wonders; no love for the future of the promised land nor for the adventures that were ahead. Dante describes them as the "dead people to whom the sea was opened."

Is this you? Are you in a pitiful condition? Don't let the vice of acedia keep you as a slave. Is God working mighty deeds around you? Don't let the vice of acedia blind you. Are you standing before a Red Sea that could lead you to a new level of adventure and passion for life? Don't let acedia keep you in the murky comfort of the Egyptian mud pits.

So if this is the disease, what is the medicine?

The mountain. The story in the mountain contains a positive example of passion. Here, Dante looks to Mary for an example of overcoming acedia. In Luke 1:39 we read that "Mary in haste ran into the mountainous area."

What was happening? Mary was living a very upsetting moment in her life: she was young, unmarried, and pregnant and she carried a vision and a secret that no one seemed to share. But her thoughts did not focus on herself, nor did she shut down and lapse into lethargy.

Immediately after the apparition of Gabriel she "hurried to the hill country" to visit Elizabeth.

Why did she go? Perhaps to share the wonder with Elizabeth, perhaps for love of her elderly relative, perhaps to protect herself and gain strength to face her calling . . . we don't know.

What we do know is that a pregnant teenage girl packed her bags, hiked up a rocky path into the hilly countryside, faced the dangers of a journey (apparently alone) and went to visit an elderly woman.

Could this be you? In the intense moments of your life, can you find the will to not think only of yourself, but to choose to direct your love to others and to God's plans? Can you find determination in your footsteps as Mary did in climbing the hilly countryside?

Yes, with the help of God you can. You can "hurry" just like Mary. You can have plans, objectives, and passionately pursue the calling of God on your life.

Now respond: In his poem, Dante cures those whose sin is acedia by having them continually run to make up for lost time. As a disciple of Christ, are you in the habit of losing time? Much time today can be lost on social media and on watching endless movie series. These can contribute to habits of acedia. Of course, there is nothing wrong with relaxing or with good entertainment, but there are insidious excesses. Do you binge on movie series because you are bored? Do you take refuge in social media to shut the world out and "be left alone"?

If you know that you are losing time, write some concrete actions below to replace bad habits with good habits.

🙏 A Prayer

Lord keep my heart and soul from the cold silence of acedia. Remove from me the desire to be left alone and to close myself off from love. May I be like young Mary, making haste to that which is next in my life as a good steward of the time you have given to me.

This week you have focused on the vice of acedia and on the virtue of passion. Next week you will look at the theological virtues of love, faith and hope.

Date completed: _____

Week 22

Being Loving, Faithful and Hopeful

See the theological virtues in your life

As we draw towards the end of this intensive stage, we come to the theological virtues. These are the three virtues that we find in 1 Corinthians 13: faith, hope and love. Before you engage with the content for this week, take a moment for a habituation check.

> **Habituation Check 12.** This is the twelfth week of practicing your habituation plan, journal below to monitor your practice.
>
> | | |
> |---|---|
> | ❏ I applied my habituation plan well this week
❏ I only marginally applied my habituation plan
❏ I forgot/was too busy to apply my habituation plan | Journal entry: |

The Theological Virtues

The virtues of *love*, *hope* and *faith* are known as the "theological virtues." Although these virtues are found in many other global traditions, the Christian theological framework has contributed to explore them in depth and bring them to a place of prominence.

The apostle Paul was the first to put these three virtues together in 1 Corinthians 13:13, indicating them as "the things which will last." Since then, rivers of ink have flown on the theological virtues.

The Virtue of Love

God is love. Since we are made in his image, it is not surprising that love is so highly acclaimed as a virtue, not only in Christianity, but in all mankind. In Confucianism, for example, love is seen as a foundational virtue. This is reflected in the famous passage called *shu*: "What you do not want others to do to you, do not do to others." Likewise, the contemporary political philosopher John Rawls claims that the virtue of love is the fundamental glue for toleration and social cohesion.

No one has made the prominence of love clearer that Jesus himself, as he indicated that the greatest commandment has to do with loving God and our neighbour (Mark 12:29–31). He also pointed out that the distinctive feature of his disciples was to be found in their love for each other (John 13:34–35). This is developed more fully in the letter of 1 John where we are told what love is, why we are to love God and our brothers and what the consequences are if we do not have love. But the most famous text on love is surely 1 Corinthians 13, where Paul describes what love is and why it is the greatest of all the things that will last.

The wealth of New Testament teaching on love is reflected in the Christian tradition that places love as the virtue that holds all other virtues to account. Augustine, for example, defined virtue and vice in terms of ordered or disordered love. For him, all virtue is well-ordered love, whereas all vice is disordered love, either in relation to God, to our neighbour or to the world. Another great theologian in the Christian tradition, Thomas Aquinas, elaborated on the centrality of the virtue of love, claiming that love is virtue that elevates and perfects all natural virtues, and that any other virtue is false unless it is motivated by love.

Love is like a fertile woman, laden with children, who loves and serves all life. Love is moved by a warming passion and by the generous giving of oneself to the good of people, projects, things and principles with the same intensity that we commit to our own welfare. Love is the embodiment of the golden rule of doing to others what we would have others do to us.

Love includes *solidarity* towards neighbours and enemies in need. It includes *friendship* and most other virtues, like *loyalty, courage, justice* and *compassion.* Love also includes *benevolence,* that is rooted in a deep satisfaction in what you have that allows you to be happy for what others have and to want their conditions to improve even further. Benevolence, in turn is related to *kindness, gentleness* and *altruism.*

Although love is directed primarily towards people, it is also directed towards structures, nature, goodness and beauty. We are called to love our neighbours, but we are also called to love our neighbourhood and creation. Hence the virtue of *civility* is related to love, as is the care for art and culture, and all virtuous actions associated with the care of our planet.

The vices-by-defect that oppose love include *envy, jealousy, pride, malevolence, indifference, exploitation, egoism, wrath* and *vengeance.* A spirit of *competition, suspicion* of other's motives, *harshness* and *cynicism* are also vices opposing love.

Love has no excesses.

The Virtue of Faith

One way to reflect on the virtue of *faith* is through its triple dispositions of reliance, reliability and loyalty.

Faith as reliance has to do with faith that you have *in* somebody or something. It is an attitude of trusting based on the conviction that the object of our faith is trustworthy. As a Christian, your faith is primarily in God, but you may also have faith in your church, in your family, in your leaders, in a cause or in your friends. Faith as reliance includes the disposition to *believe* in reliable sources and to choose to act on the basis of those beliefs. In the Bible, Abraham is seen as the champion of this kind of faith as he heard the voice of God, believed and obeyed. Faith of this kind finds its synonyms in trust and obedience.

Faith can also be seen in *faith as reliability* which has to do with faith that others can have *towards you.* It is not so much about "having faith in someone else" but about "being faithful for someone else." Faith as reliability is a gift that you give others to assure them that they can count on you because you are a trustworthy object of their faith. Those that will want to place their faith in you may include your fellow disciples, your spouse or children and the members of your community.

Faith of this second kind is about being *genuine* and *trustworthy*, and hence includes the virtue of *truthfulness* as the disposition of saying the truth (in love). Truthfulness deserves special mention because nothing will segregate social bonds as much as dishonesty. Faith as reliability is exercised through the virtues of being *responsible*, *accountable* and *answerable* for what we have, or have not, said and done, whatever the consequences. The virtue of *honesty* also finds a place here, where our words and intentions match our actions out of self-respect, respect for others, integrity and sincerity.

Faith as loyalty is a third disposition of faith that has to do with being faithful *towards* somebody or something. It is marked by *constancy* in your commitment and is an irreplaceable mark of *friendship*. But loyalty is also marked by dedication to a cause, sometimes even at the cost of your life. The martyrs are a reminder of this kind of faith.

Faith as reliance, reliability and loyalty are connected. As we exercise faith in somebody or something, we find the grounds for being trustworthy and committed to people and causes.

Faith regularly requires the exercise of prudence as we seek the mean between the vices-by-excess of *ingenuity, gullibility, over-reliance, fanaticism* and *partisanship* on the one hand and the vices-by-defect of *betrayal, distrust, cynicism, anarchy, falsehood, lying, deceit* and *dishonesty* on the other.

The Virtue of Hope

In the Christian vision, *hope* is inextricably bound with divine providence and the conviction that the future is in the hands of a loving and powerful God. This becomes a source of serenity for the believer.

More generally, hope is the habit of looking upwards and onwards. This means that hope wins over short-sightedness and the tendency to get discouraged when we are in difficulty, when we witness injustice, when our friends fail us or when we don't obtain the results we have worked for. Hope is a virtue that projects us towards a positive future and enriches our life with an optimistic outlook.

Hope is closely linked to the virtue of *joy*, as a choice to smile and not be overwhelmed by adverse circumstances.

Patience is virtue that relates to hope as it invites appropriate expectations regarding the evils of the world and its inhabitants. The virtue of patience might be described as the disposition to bear conflicts, to resolve difficulties in peace over time, to put up with the deficiencies of those around us, and to allow time to pass before finding solutions. Patience is the opposite of *wrath* that explodes during conflict. Patience is the precious ability to remain controlled and to know how to wait, demonstrating wise discernment between the excesses of *irascibility*, *intemperance*, *impulsiveness* and *haste* and the deficiencies of *resignation* and *defeatism*.

Hope however needs discernment in order to avoid the excess of *ingenuity*, *gullibility* and *insensitivity*. These can be cruel vices, especially when they are exercised in the light of pain and suffering. We need to take care, for example, in lightly prescribing optimism to those that are in difficulty, understanding that there are times in which we need simply offer hospitality to the suffering of others during the dark valleys of life.

The main vice-by-defect of hope is found in *cynicism*, a sad vice that loses all hope in people and in the future and presents life as dark and despairing.

An Animal Story

Inspiration about virtue can be found in animals, and the true story of the dog Hachikō is a wonderful example of love, faith and hope (see also the movie *A Dog's Tale*).[60]

In November 1923, an Akita puppy was born in a barn in Odate, Japan. In 1924, the puppy was given to a man with whom he would forge an incredible, unshakable bond.

Ueno Hidesaburo was a professor in the Department of Agriculture at the Imperial University of Tokyo (now The University of Tokyo). Not in the market for a pup, Ueno unexpectedly accepted Hachikō as a gift from his former student. In the winter of 1924 Hachikō arrived in Tokyo to meet Ueno. A fragile pup in poor health, Hachikō slept under Ueno's Western-style bed, wrapped in fabric (in those days it was rare to find dogs indoors). Hachikō became weaker and developed a fever, causing Ueno and his wife to bolster their efforts to nurse him back to health.

Once healed, every morning Hachikō accompanied Ueno to Shibuya Station where the two would part ways for the day. Rain or snow, Hachikō would return to the station to greet his beloved companion at the end of each day. Their routine continued for years, and provided constant comfort and unwavering friendship. On 21 May 1925, Hachikō watched his friend Professor Ueno board the train for the last time. That day, while lecturing his students, the fifty-three-year-old professor suffered a fatal stroke. It would be the last day Hachikō ever saw the professor again.

When Ueno died, his wife could not keep a large dog like Hachikō so she sent him to live with a relative who lived in Asakusa, in the eastern part of Tokyo. Despite the distance, Hachikō would repeatedly run back to his former house in Shibuya. Concerned for the dog's health and safety, the professor's former gardener, Kikusaburo Kobayashi, took Hachikō in, having known Hachikō for years. The dog longed for his owner, and every morning, he returned to the train station to wait for Ueno.

Although Hachikō was not a stray, people around the station assumed he was – why else would a dog be there by himself? As such, some of the employees treated him poorly. They would paint his face with a moustache and children would tease and taunt. Vendors even went so far as to pour water on Hachikō, hoping it would make him leave and not return. He was seen as a nuisance – an abandoned, unwanted beast. When one of Ueno's students, Hirokichi Saito, recognized Hachikō, he attempted to stop the abuse. He contacted a local media outlet, who published a story which gained instant traction and spread throughout Japan.

Hachikō's years on the street had left him battle-scarred and underweight. One of his ears drooped and he suffered from severe heartworms. But still Hachikō spent most of his days sprawled out on the station ground, eyes still searching for his master. On 7 March 1935, a station employee noticed Hachikō walking into secluded rooms and going into shops where he had been treated kindly, perhaps looking for a familiar face. He was last seen asleep on a wooden bed by the baggage room. The next day he was found dead on the side of the road.

Hachikō had waited for almost ten years for the professor. On 10 March 1935, a small memorial was held at Hachikō's shrine which was located next to Ueno's resting place. Hachikō's death made front page news, and the people of Japan deeply mourned his passing. Schools in Japan often cited Hachikō to their students as an example of loyalty, friendship and good character.

Today, we can see in this wonderful dog an example of the virtues of love, faith and hope.

Verify

Verify your understanding of the theological virtues.[61]

(a) The virtues of faith, hope and love are exclusive to Christianity.   ☐ True ☐ False

(b) The virtues of faith, hope and love are specifically developed in Christian thought and practice.   ☐ True ☐ False

(c) Who defined all virtue in terms of "well-ordered love"? _____

(d) Who said that love elevates and perfects all other virtues? _____

(e) Faith can have the dispositions of _____,
_____ and _____.

(f) List two other virtues that are closely associated with hope:

_____, _____.

Act: Asking for Infused Virtue

Christian theologians have suggested that theological virtues are "infused" by God into the life of the believer by grace. Whereas the moral virtues may be obtained by human effort and habituated with our will, the theological virtues of faith, hope and love are seen primarily as gifts of God.

The action for this week has therefore to do with prayer. In the space below, write a prayer in which you ask God to bless you with more faith, more hope, more love.

As with all divine gifts, faith, hope and love need to be cultivated. So, as you ask for these in prayer, also make a commitment to consciously develop these virtues in your life of discipleship.

⊤ Bible Study: The Greatest of All

Read: 1 Corinthians 13

The words of Paul on the "three things that last" represent the primary text that relates to the theological virtues of faith, hope and love.

Although this is likely a familiar passage to you, you may have never considered it through the lens of virtue. Think for a moment about what you have learned in general about the virtues.

You have learned that virtue is a "stable disposition concerned with praiseworthy functioning in significant and distinctive spheres of human life." Does this apply to the theological virtues? Faith is a distinctive sphere in your life. Hope is a stable disposition that you aim to have. Love is the most praiseworthy of all functions.

You have learned that virtue shapes our character. Can you see how this is true for the theological virtues? Faith shapes your attention and bends your will. Hope changes your emotions and determines your desires. Love influences your expression as a result of deep stable change in your character.

You have learned that virtue bears good fruits. And so it is with the theological virtues. They enable you to flourish and perform better. They improve the world around you. They are marks of Christian discipleship which, as the text reminds us, give meaning to everything else.

Let us come back now to the text, with a special focus on love which is its main subject. We find that Paul unpacks the virtue of love through other related virtues and vices. Read the text and write the verses that match the following list:

Patience _____	Goodness _____
Jealousy _____	Vainglory _____
Honour of others _____	Selflessness and generosity _____
Bitterness _____	Criticism _____
Justice _____	Truthfulness _____

Now respond: There are other virtues in 1 Corinthians 13 that were intentionally not included in the list above. Can you find them and write them in the box below? Also make a note of which of the virtues in 1 Corinthians 13 you find most challenging.

 A Prayer

Lord, grant me love. May I not be a resounding gong without it. May I be something because I have it. May I gain something because I give it.

> This week you have built your virtue literacy by focusing on the
> theological virtues of faith, hope and love. Next week you will look
> at the final virtue in this intensive stage: the virtue of prudence.

Date completed: _____

Week 23

Being Prudent

See this cardinal meta-virtue in your life

This is the last week in your intensive practice. This week you will meet with your character friend for your final scheduled meeting and conclude your habituation plan.

Habituation Check 13. This is the last week of practicing your habituation plan, journal below to monitor your practice.

❏ I applied my habituation plan well this week ❏ I only marginally applied my habituation plan ❏ I forgot/was too busy to apply my habituation plan	Journal entry:

Prudence: The "Tool-Belt" Virtue

It is appropriate to conclude your intensive practice stage with a capstone virtue: the virtue of *prudence*.

The virtue of prudence is one of the four cardinal virtues (the other three being *temperance*, *courage* and *justice*). But prudence also stands in a category of its own as a meta-virtue that governs all the rest.

The virtue of prudence is frequently misunderstood. The term "prudence" depending on linguistic translations, can be mistaken with the habit of "being careful." But this is not the true meaning of prudence, which is much broader. The Latin term *prudentia* means "looking ahead with wisdom" and Greek term *phronesis* is even broader, involving wisdom, intelligence and good judgement in all things related to our actions, character and habits.

Prudence is often depicted in ancient art as someone looking into a mirror, indicating an effort to see yourself as you truly are and what you truly want to be in each circumstance.

A good metaphor to understand prudence is that of a handyman's belt. Imagine the different virtues as tools that hang on a belt. You, as a handyman, need to continually choose which tool to use depending on what task is at hand. For one task, you may select a pair of pliers, for another a hammer and for another yet a screwdriver. You cannot use all the tools at the same time, and you need to be continually making choices. How then is that choice made? It is though the virtue of prudence, which is the virtue that helps you identify which virtue should be used at the appropriate time.

That is why it is called a meta-virtue, because it stands outside of the other virtues and helps you discern which ones to use.

Here are some examples. Prudence helps the soldier decide when it is time for courage and when it is time for patience. Prudence helps the care-worker know when it is time for compassion and when it is time for truthfulness. Prudence helps the leader discern when it is time for humility and when ambition is called for. Prudence guides you in choosing whether to express words of hope to alleviate the pain of your neighbour or offer silent hospitality to their suffering.

In the words of Ecclesiastes, prudence helps you discern when it is time to sow and when it is time to reap, when it is time to laugh and when to cry, when it is time to gather and when to scatter.

Prudence also allows you to discern how much, and what expression of each virtue is fitting for each circumstance. The virtues, in fact, are not simple mechanisms that you automatically turn on and off and that you always express in exactly the same way. Being virtuous is an art, and the virtue of prudence helps you paint harmonious pictures that skilfully adapt to the circumstances of life.

Here are some more examples. Prudence helps you when you are in a situation of conflict to discern the right balance between saying firm words of justice and exercising self-control to remain silent. Prudence accompanies you in a new sporting challenge and allows you to enjoy a balanced passion in light of the challenge without going overboard and forfeiting your diligence towards your existing duties. Prudence helps you in educating your children to search for right combinations between discipline and orderliness on the one hand and relaxation and freedom on the other.

As you have seen over the last weeks, the virtues can go wrong either by excess or by defect. But how do you know when you are leaning towards excess or toward defect? Again, it is prudence that helps you find the golden mean in each given situation.

Can you now see how prudence is important and how it operates in regulating and applying all of the other virtues?

The Opposing Vices

The vices that oppose prudence are *cleverness*, which gives the appearance of wisdom but has no substance; *negligence*, which gives up on seeking the best in every situation; *stupidity*, which always does the same things in every circumstance; and *over-simplicity*, which is content with quick, superficial solutions based on hearsay, uncritical imitation of others around us or poorly reasoned opinions.

Fixation is the vice whereby we find one way of doing something, and then always and only do it in that way. This can give us a sense of security, but it leads to mindless repetition and can create great damage, much as what would happen by beating a screw with a hammer that instead requires a screwdriver.

Prudence cannot exist in a vacuum and, as with all the virtues, needs to be balanced by other virtues. So, for example, if you are prudent and are not also compassionate and loving, your prudence will turn into the vice of *cunning*, which is finding ways to benefit only oneself.

Do any of these vices describe you? If they do, and if your score in the Virtue Test was low in this virtue, then you may want to choose to work on the virtue of prudence in your character.

A Story of Prudence

The story of prudence this week comes from the Bible and is the story of when Jesus visits Martha and Mary in Bethany.

Begin by taking a few moments to observe the story as seen in the painting of Johannes Vermeer. Scan the QR code below to view it.

(*Christ in the House of Martha and Mary* – Johannes Vermeer – Wikipedia)[62]

As Jesus shows up in the home of Mary and Martha with his hungry disciples, Mary sits at the feet of Jesus, while Martha is "distracted" with the preparations that need to be made to feed everyone.

This story has often been used to conclude that Mary is better than Martha. That contemplative virtues are *always* superior to the service virtues. That thinking is *always* better than doing. That learning *always* comes before acting. That faith *always* comes before works. That spiritual things are *always* superior to material things. But is that the true teaching of this story?

If we look carefully at Martha, she is actually an impressive example of virtue. She exhibits virtues that every Christian should have. She is happy to give, for she is convinced that Jesus is the Messiah. The sacredness of hospitality is on her mind, together with empathy for a group of men who are hungry and have been walking around the country. There is a spirit of generosity about her which we sometimes find in people of wealth. She is absolving a duty of care, even showing great flexibility, as the visit may have been unannounced. She shows industry, initiative and responsibility as she saw the "preparations that had to be made" (40) – you can easily see in her the woman of virtue in Proverbs 31. She also sees injustice, and I think any of us would have been justly annoyed with the disparity of work allocation. So there are plenty of good things to learn about Martha.

But, in *this* story, Mary is praised as the one who has "made the better choice." Is this *always* the case? No. We can find plenty of other narratives in the Bible that praise service, that call us to hospitality, that say that true religion is taking care of orphans and widows and that tell us to be like industrious ants.

So what is the issue here? Where did Martha go wrong?

She lacked prudence.

Martha was not "wrong" in her virtues, she was wrong in the choice of virtue in this circumstance. Jesus only had a few more months before the passion, and at this time, in this circumstance, eating was not the highest priority. She wasn't wrong, she was inappropriate.

Martha's deep problem, which Jesus points out, is not lack of direction, but lack of balance. Not fault in choosing, but inflexibility is changing.

And so it is for you. Even the best life of virtue, if not regulated by prudence, can lead you down the wrong pathway.

✅ Verify

This lesson might have introduced some new concepts around prudence. Before proceeding, briefly verify your understanding.[63]

(a) Prudence is the meta-virtue among the four Cardinal virtues.

☐ True
☐ False

(b) Prudence means "being careful."

☐ True
☐ False

(c) Prudence is that practical wisdom that helps you discern which virtues are necessary as you meet life's unpredictable circumstances.

☐ True
☐ False

(d) Prudence is called a _____ because it stands outside of the other virtues and helps you discern which ones to use and in which measure.

(e) Always doing the same things in the same way in every circumstance can be the vice of _____.

(f) This is the final week of intensive practice. I have habituated for thirteen weeks, met with my character friend(s) five times (including this week) and built my virtue literacy around ten virtues.

☐ Yes
☐ No
☐ Mostly

Act: Engage Your Character Friend

This week you will need to meet with your friend for the fifth and final time. Write the time/date of your meeting in the box below:

If you are working with a group, a meeting with your Character Friend Triplet will be part of your weekly group meeting, so you do not need to plan it separately.

Here is a suggested outline for your final time together with your character friend:

1. Give account of your habituation plan both for this week, but also overall over the last 3 months.

2. Talk about the virtue of prudence that you have considered this week and discuss examples of what this might look like in each other's lives. In particular, look back over the last months of intensive practice and try to pinpoint exact instances in which you exercised prudence. Or where you did not.

3. Ask your character friend for general feedback on your character and whether/how you have grown in the last weeks.

4. As this is the final meeting, take some time to assess your character friendship relationship and your regular meetings. What worked well? How did you benefit? What might have improved? How would your journey of growth in character and virtue have been without a character friend?

5. Also decide on whether you want to continue to be accountable to each other and in what ways.

Give a brief account of the final meeting with your character friend in the box below:

Bible Study: Stories of Honey and Fools

Read: Proverbs 24:13, 25:16 and 26:4–5

Proverbs might be called "the book of prudence." Starting from the first chapter, we read proverb after proverb that is intended to give wisdom and instruction, inform prudent behaviour and help the reader in doing what is right and just.

In line with the true nature of prudence, Proverbs is not simply a list of things that everyone needs to do, all the time, in the same way, in every circumstance. Rather, it points to the kind of people we should be. And this often requires doing things differently in different circumstances.

Here are two examples.

Honey. In Proverbs 24:13 we find that we should eat honey, because it is good. If that is all we read, we might establish that there is a standard behaviour of what it means to be a wise person. A wise person is someone that, every time they find some honey, they eat it. But we need to read more. Because in Proverbs 25:16 we find a counterpoint, that tells us that, if we find honey, we should "eat just enough" and not too much or we will vomit.

So our relationship with honey is not straightforward and mindless. We cannot simply just eat. We need to be prudent to understand what "too much" means. In this case, prudence regulates the virtue of enjoyment with moderation.

Fools. In Proverbs 26 we find instructions on what to do when we come into contact with fools. In Proverbs 26:4 we are told that we should "not answer a fool according to his folly, or you yourself will be just like him." This is wonderful advice that tells us that when a fool talks to us, we should exercise the virtue of restraint and remain silent, refusing to align our conversation with the conversation of the fool. In ignoring fools in this way, we avoid being foolish ourselves.

But should we always adopt this same strategy?

No. We read, in fact, in Proverbs 26:5 that we should "answer a fool according to his folly, or he will be wise in his own eyes." But wait a moment. This is now saying the exact opposite of what the previous proverb said. We are being told that when a fool talks to us, we are not to remain silent, but to reply along the lines of their conversation. As we do this, we help the fool see how foolish they actually are.

So in the light of these conflicting instructions, how do we know which behaviour to follow? Prudence will guide us. If we are wise, we will know that there is more than one appropriate kind of response. And then our prudent character will express itself rightly in the specific instance. There will be times in which we will exercise the virtue of self-control and remain silent. Then there will be times in which we will exercise the virtue of irony and speak out. We cannot do both at the same time. We need prudence.

Is this too complicated? If you are a Christian, there is good news. Part of the richness of grace that God has given us in Christ, includes abundance of "all wisdom and prudence (*phronesis*)" (Ephesians 1:8 KJV).

Now respond: Is there something that you do, all the time, in the same way, in every circumstance? Might this lesson on prudence have led you to reconsider that there might be other ways?

In the box below, write this out together with one practical action of doing something differently.

 A Prayer

Lord, help me to accept that the complexities of life may require me to be and act differently. Keep me from being simple-minded and allow me to joyfully engage with the challenges of prudence. Thank you for the guiding voice of your Spirit in my life, and may I be receptive and responsive to the ongoing call of wisdom.

> This has been the final week of your intensive practical session. You have concluded your habituation project, met with your character friend(s) for a final evaluation meeting, and increased your virtue literacy by focusing on the virtue of prudence. Next week you will evaluate your progress and celebrate your character growth.

Date completed: _____

Week 24

Evaluate, Reflect and Celebrate

Final steps in your character and virtue education project

In this final week of your character and virtue education project you will review your progress, celebrate your growth and make new plans.

The reflective writing exercise that you will be asked to complete this week may take one or two hours to produce, so you may need to set aside a little more time than usual.

Take the Virtue Test Again

In order to help you evaluate your character growth, you will now take the Virtue Test again. This should take about twenty minutes as before. When you are done, come back to this page to interpret your results.

(Virtue Test)[64]

After completing the Virtue Test you will see your new score. Please record these scores in the Second Test column of the table below.

Now go back to Week 6 and write your previous results in the First Test column above.

	First Test	Second Test	Better, Same or Worse?
Your score in virtue of PRUDENCE	_____	_____	_____
Your score in virtue of TEMPERANCE	_____	_____	_____
Your score in virtue of COURAGE	_____	_____	_____
Your score in virtue of JUSTICE	_____	_____	_____
Your score in virtue of HUMILITY	_____	_____	_____
Your score in virtue of CONSTANCY	_____	_____	_____
Your score in virtue of TRUTHFULNESS	_____	_____	_____
Your score in virtue of COMPASSION	_____	_____	_____
Your score in virtue of FAITH	_____	_____	_____
Your score in virtue of HOPE	_____	_____	_____
Your score in virtue of LOVE	_____	_____	_____
Your score in virtue of DILIGENCE	_____	_____	_____
Your score in virtue of KNOWLEDGE	_____	_____	_____

Compare the two columns and in the final column Better, Same or Worse put a "+" for all scores that have improved, an "=" sign for all scores that are virtually the same and a "–" sign for all scores that are lower.

Here is an example of what a line in the completed table might look like.

Now look in particular at the score of the virtue that you have been working on in your habituation plan. Is this score better, the same or worse? Write this below:

	First Test	Second Test	Better, Same or Worse?
Your score in virtue of COURAGE	67	82	+

Interpret your results

There are different possible outcomes as you compare these scores.

In my second test, the score in the virtue I have been habituating is:	❑ Better ❑ The Same ❑ Worse

Outcome 1: Your second score is higher than the first

Clearly, this is the desired outcome which will (hopefully) be most frequent. If you have scored higher in the virtue that you have been habituating, you can take this as a marker of successful virtue education.

This is great news, and you should be encouraged! Although numerical results are not perfect and self-evaluation tests are far from accurate, a positive comparison of this kind is a good indication that your character has been positively educated in virtue. This means that habituation, character friends and virtue literature have worked to make your character more virtuous than before.

Outcome 2: Your second score is lower than (or equal to) the first
This could mean several things.

1. You may have tested yourself with greater severity. It is possible that, as you have become more aware of virtue in the last months, you have become harsher in your answers. This will distort the comparison and make it look like you have not grown in virtue, whereas in actual fact you have.

2. The test has not worked for you. Tests can go wrong in many ways, and you should not be discouraged by the numbers. If you perceive that you have grown in this virtue, that is what counts, regardless of numerical results.

3. You have actually not grown in virtue. This is a possibility, and if it is true you need to take responsibility for it. Perhaps you were not constant in your habituation. Perhaps you did not meet with your character friends or were not sincere in your accountability. Perhaps you worked alone when you really needed a supporting community. Perhaps unpredicted events in your life distracted you from focusing on your practices. Perhaps your habituation plan was superficial or poorly designed. Or perhaps your will and motivation were not determined to really become more virtuous and less viceful. If any of these are true, take ownership for your mistakes and consider re-engaging with the process with greater care.

4. Your growth in virtue is not showing . . . yet. This means that you are travelling in the right direction, but you need more time. It could be that your habituation period was not long enough. But it is also possible that you have chosen to work on a particularly challenging virtue, or on a vice that is deeply embedded in your life. In this case, true change will require more time. So don't give up, results may come slowly and after more work! You are on the right pathway, but it is longer and more difficult than you had anticipated.

Hopefully, comparing the scores of your Virtue Test has been encouraging.

Verify

In this final verification section, ensure you have understood the results of your Virtue Tests.[65]

(a) The Virtue Test is infallible.	❏ True ❏ False
(b) If I scored higher in the second test, it is a good indication of character growth.	❏ True ❏ False
(c) If I scored the same or lower in the second test, there are several possible reasons that I need to evaluate.	❏ True ❏ False

Act: Write Reflectively on Your Growth

You have nearly completed this character and virtue education plan. It is now time to consolidate your growth through a short piece of reflective writing.

You may feel like you have already achieved much. And that is true, for if you have been constant in your practice plan, you have indeed achieved much. But there is something about reflective writing that consolidates this experience in your memory.

The benefits of reflective writing include:

- An enhanced ability to consciously focus on your growth
- A better understanding of how you have moved from weakness to strength
- A sense of encouragement and achievement
- A stronger commitment to the process of virtue education
- Unpredictable thoughts on where you can improve next

Is not an hour or two of your time worth reaping these benefits?

You may think: Why bother writing? Is it not the same thing to simply go for a nice walk and reflect in my mind about my growth? No, it is not. There is something about the slowness of writing, the forced clarity of putting words on paper and the sense of completeness of a manuscript, that has a much greater impact.

Length is not an issue, and your piece of reflective writing can be as long or as short as you want. Feel free to choose whatever style works best for you, whether a set of bullet points, spontaneous writing or taking advantage of the set of questions below. Whatever you do, give yourself the time to gain clarity and insight as you progress and do not yield to the temptation of shortcuts. You will be surprised by the benefits of this activity.

Here are some guidance questions to help you in this exercise. Boxes are provided for your responses, but feel free to write elsewhere.

1. Provide a brief narrative of what you did, starting with your self-evaluation, your choice of a virtue and your habituation plan.

2. Describe the results of your two Virtue Tests. Did the comparison of the "before and after" match your own perception of growth (or not) in virtue?

3. Write down one or two anecdotes (stories) from your experience in the last months that illustrate how you have intentionally grown in virtue.

236 Character and Virtue in Practice

4. What helped you grow? What would have helped more? What was the most difficult part? How did your habituation go? What might you do to improve next time?

5. Now go back and read the outcomes of virtue education again in Lesson 1. Try writing about the following:

- How has my attention been shaped? Do I notice more and attend more frequently to situations that require specific virtues?
- How have my emotions changed? Do I have more feelings related to virtue or vice?
- How have my desires been shaped? Do I want more virtue? Do I want to see more virtue in the world around me?
- How has my will to action been impacted? Am I doing more things that are virtuous?
- Have there been any changes in my expression, meaning that others are perceiving virtue in me?

6. You have chosen to follow this character and virtue education plan as part of your commitment to discipleship. How has this experience enhanced your walk with Christ, your relationship with God and your life in the Christian community to which you belong?

7. If you were to recommend this growth plan to someone else, what would you say?

Now Celebrate

On the seventh day of creation, God rested. He looked back on what he had accomplished and enjoyed how good it was. And then he told us to do the same.

When you complete something, you should take the time to rest and celebrate. Many of us are not too good at that. We are driven by projects and by work, and we rarely rest and celebrate. But to rest and celebrate is also an expression of virtue, and it is viceful not to do so.

So, do something to celebrate your achievement in character and virtue education. You may not have achieved all that you wanted to, but if you are reading this page, you have achieved something, and you should focus on that.

How you celebrate is entirely up to you. But make it something unusual and special. Cook a special meal. Go for a short trip somewhere. Buy yourself something that you've wanted for a while. Get a picture framed and hang it on your wall.

Write in the box below how you will celebrate.
Whatever you do to celebrate, do it looking back and saying to yourself: "Well done, this has been very good."

What Next?

Virtue education is not something that you do once and get it over with. It is a lifestyle of commitment to intentional growth. So don't stop here. Make some plans for what you would like to do next.

1.   Have you noticed another virtue that you would like to work on? Undertake the habituation and character friendships process described in Weeks 10–23 again, perhaps choosing to do your own research in different virtues for the virtue literacy tool.

2.   Would you like to share the opportunity of growth with others by leading a group of friends or fellow disciples in the process you have just completed? Seek out this opportunity.

3.   Do you want to read more about virtue? Check out some of the Further Exploration resources or simply start looking and doing research about virtue, for there is much more.

(Further Exploration)[66]

You may also feel a little tired at this point and you don't really want to plan anything quite yet. That's fine. Come back to this later.

Conclusion

This workbook has been designed to lead you through a practical plan to nourish virtuous character. Its core objective has been not to just inform you but to help form your character according to virtue.

Hopefully your experience has been one of transformation, where you have deepened your walk of discipleship, flourished as a human being and begun to perform better in key areas of your life.

But most importantly, as you have grown in character and virtue, you have contributed to improve the world around you and you have glorified God. And in so doing you have obeyed the great commandments of loving God and loving your neighbour.

Your Feedback

As the author of this workbook, I'd like to thank you for joining this journey into virtue. If you'd like to contact me, I'd be happy to reply to you by email contact@virtueducation.net

Please take a few minutes to provide your feedback on your experience of growth in character and virtue here:

(Your Feedback)[67]

If, in time, you come across resources concerning character and virtue education in your context and culture that might be useful to others, feel free to use the feedback form to share these with the author.

In this final week you have taken the Virtue Test again and
compared your scores to evaluate your growth. You have
consolidated your growth through a piece of reflective writing.
Finally, you have celebrated and thought about next steps.

Date completed: _____

Group Facilitator Guidelines

Although the growth plan outlined in this workbook can work for individual use, it works best when done in communities such as small discipleship groups, regular church meetings, non-formal training programme clusters or cohorts of students in formal theology programmes.

A key to the success of these groups is the way they are facilitated, and this final section offers a step-by-step guide for group leaders.

Before starting to use the specific week-by-week guidelines below, here are some general suggestions.

1. Lead differently. Leading a group in a character and virtue education project is a peculiar task and you need to tailor your leadership style accordingly. This is not a set of lectures or a Bible study where you as a leader talk most of the time and then participants ask you questions. Nor is it a prayer or therapy group where everyone has a turn to talk about what is happening in their lives. It is a group of like-minded adults that have independently decided to work on their character and to be accountable to each other.

2. Lead as a guide-on-the-side. Since each person in your group has made a personal commitment to grow in virtue, there is a sense in which everyone is self-led, self-motivated and responsible for themselves. Your role as a group facilitator is not to drive the herd, nor to stand up and call others to follow you. You are there to facilitate, coordinate and to create a context of accountability.

3. Consider the size of your group. This kind of project may not work well in a very large group. If you have more than a dozen or so participants in your group, you might consider having more than one group.

4. Make the best use of the written materials in this workbook. Each participant has access to the same materials as you do and will be engaging in personal study before the group meetings. This means that you need to build on this during the meetings and not repeat the content of the activities. In educational terms, this is a "flipped classroom" approach.

In terms of our own preparation to facilitate the group, here are two further suggestions:

1. Prepare by reading the companion volume *Character and Virtue in Theological Education* (Marvin Oxenham, 2019, Langham Global Library). This book will help you understand in greater depth the theories and practices of character and virtue education and provide you with additional insight to share during the group meetings.

2. Go through the twenty-four-week plan in this workbook yourself, so you can speak from experience. You can either do this before you begin facilitating a group or together with your first group as a fellow participant.

3. Remember to regularly check the Further Exploration page (see QR code below) to enrich your meetings with other possible resources.

(Further Exploration)[68]

On the following pages you will find a list of suggestions for each group meeting. They are arranged to match the twenty-four weeks in the workbook. Notice, that these are not prescriptive lists of activities, but ideas that you can choose from. What you choose to do will depend on the nature of your group, on the time you have available, on the desired outcome and on your personal contribution as a leader.

Week 1 – Facilitator Guide

(to be used in conjunction with Week 1 in this workbook)

This is your first meeting with the group. Introductions may be required. Ask participants about their fears and expectations as they embark in a character and virtue growth project.

Take some time to ensure everyone understands how things work. You may need to consult the Introduction chapter again to ensure that as a group leader you understand the project well. Give some time for questions on what this is all about. Participants may be used to meeting in a group to be taught, or to pray and have fellowship together. But this is different, as it is a character growth project that the group will be working through together over twenty-four weeks.

If participants have not read the materials in Week 1, take turns simply reading sections and then pause to allow for comment. Then lead discussion around the questions for understanding in the Verify section (fifteen minutes). If participants have already read the materials, lead them directly into a discussion.

From the Bible study, look at the lists of ten vices and seven virtues. Did participants get these right? Which of these represent a challenge?

Give time alone for each group member to write a prayer expressing desire to grow in virtue. Then have a time of collective prayer.

Homework. The growth project assumes that all participants will complete the lesson for each week before the group meeting. This will allow for better participation. So, before their next meeting, remind participants to complete Week 2 in their workbook on their own. If you are not meeting weekly as a group, you may need to adjust this provision, but try to maintain the same dynamic of individual preparation before each group meeting.

Check the Further Exploration section for additional resources for this week.

(Further Exploration)[69]

Your notes for this meeting:

Week 2 – Facilitator Guide

(to be used in conjunction with Week 2 in this workbook)

This is your second group meeting so it may be good to repeat what your group is about, the objectives of the plan and how you will be organising yourself.

Ask participants if they have completed the lesson for this week on their own. Encourage them to do so regularly. If participants have not read the materials, take turns simply reading sections and then pause to allow for comment.

Lead a general discussion around the questions for understanding in the Verify section.

Have everyone share what they have written in the Act section after searching the internet for the word "virtue." Discuss together what everyone discovered about character, virtue and education in your context/culture/language.

Watch the video *Add to your faith, virtue* that builds on the materials from the Bible study (twenty minutes). You can access this through the QR code below. Elaborate your own questions for discussion and have everyone share what they wrote in the Respond box about how this teaching contributes to their understanding of discipleship.

(Video of sermon by Dr Oxenham at London School of Theology)[70]

Homework. Remind participants to complete Week 3 in their workbook before your next meeting. The Bible Study in Week 3 is a little longer than usual, so you might suggest that they only complete the exercise in Romans, leaving the other exercises/texts to be completed during your group meeting next week.

Check the Further Exploration section for additional resources for this week.

(Further Exploration)[71]

Your notes for this meeting:

Week 3 – Facilitator Guide

(to be used in conjunction with Week 3 in this workbook)

Start with a brief sharing time around the following question: Before this week, would you have been able to make connections between character, virtue and the Bible? Are you convinced that these are important themes in the Bible and in church history?

Have participants share the results of the survey they conducted in the Act section. Discuss overall considerations that emerge from their conversations.

Check the matching exercise of virtues in Romans 13–16, discussing whether everyone got similar answers. In the Further Exploration resources for this week you will find a resource called the *Roman Road to Virtue.* Consider using this resource to offer the group some additional teaching about virtue in Romans. You can access this through the QR code below:

(The Roman Road to Virtue)[72]

Depending on the size of your group, make groups of three and assign to each one of the seven ethical lists that are provided in the Bible study for this week. Give them some time to complete the exercise. Then bring the larger group back together and have each sub-group share their insights from their texts.

If time allows, consider a further conversation about how the biblical accounts of the creation and the fall influence our thinking about virtue, character and the place of education.

Devotional idea. If participants would like to continue their search for virtue in the Bible, suggest that they buy a coloured pencil and keep it in their Bible. Every time they read a passage that refers to a virtue, suggest that they underline it. The result will be a growing visual representation of virtue in the Bible.

Homework. By now, participants should have acquired a pattern of completing each lesson before the next group meeting. In any case, remind them to complete Week 4.

Check the Further Exploration section for additional resources for this week.

(Further Exploration)[73]

Your notes for this meeting:

Week 4 – Facilitator Guide

(to be used in conjunction with Week 4 in this workbook)

Review the examples of various traditions of character and virtue. Leave room for questions or discussion.

Also discuss the statement "Virtue education is not just a Christian thing." How does that make everyone feel? Is there agreement? Disagreement? What is distinctive about the pursuing character and virtue as a Christian?

Provide a time for participants to share what they have found about character and virtue in your own context and culture. You may want to do some additional research as a facilitator and be prepared to share what you've found. Some ideas are found in the Further Exploration list for Week 4.

(Further Exploration)[74]

Discuss what participants have found in the Bible study on Proverbs. If they have not done this on their own, put them into small groups to complete it together. You might also want to discuss how they feel about the association that is made in the lesson between wisdom and virtue.

Conclude with a time of prayer. If there are women in the group, you may want to suggest a special focus of thanksgiving for their virtues as seen in Proverbs 31.

Your notes for this meeting:

Week 5 – Facilitator Guide

(to be used in conjunction with Week 5 in this workbook)

The main focus for the group meeting this week is on making a shared commitment to the work ahead. Consider this as a sort of commencement week. Unless participants have skimmed ahead in the workbook, they may not fully understand what is involved. Consider a very brief overview of what lies ahead.

Go through the three questions in the Bible study in Exodus on being stiff-necked. If participants have already answered them in their personal study, have them share their results. Otherwise, have the work completed in small groups and then arrange a time of sharing.

In smaller groups (to facilitate participation) have everyone share their responses to the four questions in the Act section for Week 5. Also include a conversation about the dynamics of accountability and on what this might look like in your particular group. In the larger group, you might want to read the four questions out loud and ask the group to respond out loud with a "yes I do." This will generate a communal feeling of commitment.

As participants express their commitment to character and virtue, they may fear failure and you should remind them of the God-given resources that you have seen in the previous weeks (e.g. the Spirit who frees from the bondage of sin, the divine power of the Spirit to be virtuous, etc).

If you have time, it might be interesting to create a visual reminder together. Or have participants share what they have produced.

This is a good meeting to have a time of prayer and commitment. You may want to encourage prayer that reflects the contents of the Bible studies of the previous weeks (e.g. on the imitation of Christ, on adding virtue to our faith, on the ethical list of the fruit of the Spirit or on the wisdom from Proverbs).

Homework. In the next meeting you will engage with the Virtue Test (Week 6). Participants however need to take this test at home on their own before the next meeting, so remind them to complete it.

Check the Further Exploration section for additional resources for this week.

(Further Exploration)[75]

Your notes for this meeting:

Week 6 – Facilitator Guide

(to be used in conjunction with Week 6 in this workbook)

Ideally, everyone should have taken the virtue test at home. If not, you will need to allow an extra fifteen minutes during the meeting to do so (this is not ideal as it is best to allow some time for the results of the test to mature in private).

Care needs to be taken in preparing this group meeting. The best outcome of the meeting is that participants feel free to share the results of their Virtue Test with each other. This will give a sense of community and accountability and will begin to create a context where participants can receive initial feedback from others on their character. However, depending on how the group is made up, this may not always be easily achievable. If, for example, participants do not know each other well, it may be intimidating and threatening to disclose their test results. Also, in some cultures, this kind of personal sharing may be unusual. So some discernment is needed. You may need to do some preparatory work beforehand to create group dynamics that will support this kind of sharing. The ideas listed below, need to be filtered and adapted to what is fitting for each group.

Begin with general discussion on self-assessment.

- How do participants feel about self-assessment? Do they regularly engage with it?
- Is it associated with positive or negative feelings?
- Talk about humility and prudence, doing a little more research on these virtues if needed. Why are they needed for self-assessment?
- Agree/disagree with the following statement: "If we do not begin with honest self-assessment, we will never grow in virtue."

Go through the Bible study in James. Ask participants to share what they wrote in the "Now respond" box.

Ask participants to share about the Virtue Test:

- How did they feel as they were taking it?
- Were there some questions that were not clear?
- What seem to be their strongest virtues? What seem to be their weakest virtues (and potential vices)?
- Do they feel that the test has worked for them? Do the results seem to match how they perceive themselves? (Be careful here not to discuss the results in too much detail, as that is the topic for next week.)

Homework. For next week, participants need to complete Week 7. Also challenge participants to be praying specifically that the Spirit of God would be leading them in the choice of one particular virtue on which to focus in the months to come.

Check the Further Exploration section for additional resources for this week.

(Further Exploration)[76]

Your notes for this meeting:

Week 7 – Facilitator Guide

(to be used in conjunction with Week 7 in this workbook)

Start with reflecting/summarizing the content of the Bible study *You are the Man*. Also talk about the place of repentance in discipleship.

Go through the materials together "Vices by Excess and Defect" and "Understand the Virtues" that are found in the materials for Week 7. Have participants discuss how these explanations relate to the virtue on which they scored lowest.

Give individual time during the group for each to complete the Act section and choose a virtue on which they are going to work.

Have everyone share the virtue they have selected and then have everyone pray for each other.

As a group leader, you may need to spend some personal time with each participant to clarify their chosen virtue. In particular there is the potential for confusion because whereas the Virtue Test helps identify weaknesses in given virtues, it does not distinguish well between vices-by-excess and vices-by-defect. So, someone may test low on courage, which could mean that they are too cowardly, but it might also mean that they are too reckless. This is a vital distinction and to get it wrong would mean working in exactly the opposite direction to what is needed. Some personal conversation with you may be helpful.

Homework. Participants will need to complete Week 8 before the next meeting.

Check the Further Exploration section for additional resources for this week.

(Further Exploration)[77]

Your notes for this meeting:

Week 8 – Facilitator Guide

(to be used in conjunction with Week 8 in this workbook)

This week it is important to focus on the methodology and outline of the weeks ahead. So far, this workbook has been content-rich and participants have been helped to understand some of the basics in character and virtue education. The very practical part began in Week 6 and 7 with the Virtue Test. Week 8 marks the beginning of the long, slow work of character development.

Make sure that all participants are "on the map" and understand how the coming weeks are generally organized. Provide the group with dates and deadlines that match the plan described in the diagram in Week 8.

Go over the three tools that have been introduced. At this point participants do not need to fully understand each of the tools. They will be explained further in the coming weeks. As a group leader however, you may want to read ahead to be able to answer questions if there are any.

Facilitate a discussion around intention and constancy and reinforce the image of this workbook as a training manual for a long race that will yield gradual, incremental changes.

The question raised in the Bible study on the interplay of God's work and ours in character development is important and may be controversial for some. Take time to go through the texts in Galatians together. As a group leader, you may have other relevant teaching or stories that you would like to share to reinforce this beautiful double aspect of God's work and our responsibility.

Homework. Participants will need to complete Week 9 before the next meeting.

Check the Further Exploration section for additional resources for this week.

(Further Exploration)[78]

Your notes for this meeting:

Week 9 – Facilitator Guide

(to be used in conjunction with Week 9 in this workbook)

Talk with the group about the power of habits. Give examples of good and bad habits from different areas of life. Try listing together good and bad habits in Bible characters, or in characters in famous books and movies. Ask participants to share about their own good and bad habits and try to help them see the connection between habits and character.

Discuss the Bible study about the Ten Words and the relationship between rules, virtues and character. Is character development just another form of legalism, or is it something different? Ask participants to share how they responded to associating the Ten Words with virtues (remember, there are no right answers, and each commandment can potentially be associated with more than one virtue).

Have participants share in small groups the results of the exercise for this week in which they listed activities/actions/opportunities and what habits might be developed related to their chosen virtue.

Homework. In the lesson for next week (Week 10) participants follow instructions on writing their habituation plan. It is really important that, before the next meeting, everyone has a drafted plan, because the group meeting next week will revolve around sharing these plans.

Check the Further Exploration section for additional resources for this week.

(Further Exploration)[79]

Your notes for this meeting:

Week 10 – Facilitator Guide

(to be used in conjunction with Week 10 in this workbook)

Start with the Bible study on Esther and Mordecai. If participants have completed this at home, ask them to share their response section. What would they like to imitate about Esther and Mordecai as they make plans to work on their character?

The main focus of this meeting is to have participants share their habituation plans. It is best that they come to the meeting with the plan already written out, so they have had an opportunity to think about it carefully.

Sharing habituation plans is best done in smaller groups, so there is time for everyone to share and engage.

In each small group, have each participant read their habituation plan and engage in conversation about how it responds to the eight questions listed in the Act section.

Bring the group back together and talk about the danger of forgetting, and the importance of reminder mechanisms. Ask everyone to share their own reminder strategy (creative ways? apps?). Look ahead in the workbook to the coming weeks, showing participations where the Habituation Check is each week, and making sure they understand how to use it. If there is time, talk about the practice of journaling.

Explain how your group will be of assistance in helping remember and being constant in habituation over the coming weeks.

Homework. Participants should complete the work in Week 11 before the next meeting.

Check the Further Exploration section for additional resources for this week.

(Further Exploration)[80]

Your notes for this meeting:

Week 11 – Facilitator Guide

(to be used in conjunction with Week 11 in this workbook)

This is the first week that participants have begun practicing their habituation plan. Allow some time at the beginning of the meeting for some sharing on how it went. As a starter, you might make explicit reference to the Habituation Check that will be featured at the start of each week in the workbook for the coming weeks and ask everyone to share their report for this week.

This is a good meeting during which to talk about friendship. What is friendship, how it is understood in local cultures, what different kinds of friendships are there? Go over some of the content of this lesson, focusing in particular on the distinction between utility friendships, pleasure friendships and virtue friendships. You might also ask participants to tell stories of good friendships or of lost friendship in light of the key statement "virtue is the glue of friendship."

Discuss the content of the Bible study concerning David and Jonathan. Can you think of other examples in the Bible of character friendships?

Discuss how a Christian community might function as a group of character friends. How would a church change if its fundamental function was cultivated in being a group of character friends? You might also want to deal with the touchy question of whether we all need to be friends in the same way and with the same intensity? Is jealousy between character friends a possibility? What do we do about it?

Homework. Participants should complete Week 12 before your next meeting. Instructions are given in identifying and contacting a character friend, but as a group leader you need to let your group know how character friendships will be organized in your group as this will impact the way they deal with the instructions in Week 12 (read ahead to see these). Although you can leave freedom for each participant to identify a character friend (even outside of your group), this workbook assumes that you will organize character friend triplets within the group (small groups of three). This will be explained in more detail next week but as a group leader you should prepare ahead and inform the group.

Check the Further Exploration section for additional resources for this week.

(Further Exploration)[81]

Your notes for this meeting:

Week 12 – Facilitator Guide

(to be used in conjunction with Week 12 in this workbook)

Start with a brief habituation check. How is everyone doing?

Summarize the characteristics of the friendship between David and Jonathan and ask participants to share their response sections as to what kind of character friend they would like to be.

A core element of this group meeting is to establish Character Friend Triplets (CFT). As a group leader you need to carefully establish criteria that are appropriate to your culture and context. Given the level of vulnerability and accountability that will be established within the CFT, you may need to think about issues of age and gender. In your culture, older participants may not feel comfortable about being open with younger people. Or it might work better if the groups are of the same gender. But the opposite might also be true. So, it is really up to you as a group leader to discern the best solution which might even include a random selection/extraction of the CFTs. This workbook suggests triplets as a good dynamic, but you may also have groups of two or of four.

Once you have formed/announced the CFTs give them the bulk of the meeting time to meet together. They should engage with the following tasks:

1) Each should share on their experience so far in this character growth project.

2) Each should share on the results of their Virtue Test and illustrate their habituation plan. They should also give a brief report on how the first two weeks of their habituation have gone.

3) Each should complete the Virtue Test thinking of one of the other three. Then these results should be compared with the outcome of the personal test in Week 6. This will work better if participants know each other well, but it will work relatively well in any case since the participants have been meeting together already for twelve weeks and should have begun to know each other. Use the QR code for the Virtue Test in Week 12.

Optional activity: if your group is made up of potential leaders (e.g. theology students, pastors in training, etc), you might want to initiate a discussion on the importance and strategies of cultivating character friendships in your communities.

Homework. Participants need to continue their habituation and complete the work in Week 13.

Check the Further Exploration section for additional resources for this week.

(Further Exploration)[82]

Your notes for this meeting:

Week 13 – Facilitator Guide

(to be used in conjunction with Week 13 in this workbook)

Begin the meeting with a brief time for the CFT (Character Friendship Triplets) to meet. Ask them to give an account to each other of how their habituation went this week and pray for each other.

Go through the Bible study in Philippians 4:8 again, ensuring that everyone sees the object, action and outcome in the text. Then have a time of sharing of what participants have written in the "Now respond" box in the lesson (names of characters/stories in the Bible that embody the virtues listed in Philippian 4:8). If they have not done the "negative" list of vices, this might be a good exercise to do together.

Talk more about knowledge and emulation. Explain if necessary. Ask participants to share about what books they have read/are reading that have shaped their character. Talk in general about reading novels (even secular ones) and how this might contribute to their walk of discipleship.

Conclude by going back to Week 8 and reviewing the plan for practice. All three tools have now been introduced (habituation, character friendship and virtue literacy). The next nine weeks as a group you will be using all three. It is important to regularly keep the group "on the map" of how the implementation of their character growth project is developing.

Homework. Participants should complete Week 14 before the next meeting.

Check the Further Exploration section for additional resources for this week.

(Further Exploration)[83]

Your notes for this meeting:

Week 14 – Facilitator Guide

(to be used in conjunction with Week 14 in this workbook)

Begin the meeting with a brief time for the CFT (Character Friendship Triplets) to meet. Ask them to give an account to each other of how their habituation went this week and pray for each other.

This meeting will focus on the virtue of humility, and in so doing will contribute to virtue literacy. Here are some ideas:

- Have participants share about common misconceptions of humility.
- Use the content of the lesson to try to write an anagram for the word HUMBLE in your own language.
- Questions for discussion: What other key biblical texts or stories talk about humility? Can a leader be humble and a strong, assertive leader at the same time? What other stories or famous people in your culture are examples of humility?

Have participants share what they have written in the Humility Check and how they responded to the Bible study on Mary.

If you have time, here is a further Bible study that you might share on Moses as The Most Humble Man . . .

(The Most Humble Man – https://virtueducation.net/the-most-humble-man/)

Homework. Participants will need to complete Week 15 before the next meeting.

Check the Further Exploration section for additional resources for this week.

(Further Exploration)[84]

Your notes for this meeting:

Week 15 – Facilitator Guide

(to be used in conjunction with Week 15 in this workbook)

Ask everyone in the group how their habituation is going. They have been habituating for about a month and may begin forgetting.

Begin with a summary from this lesson on what temperance is. There is some rich content in the lesson that may require further explanation or discussion. Allow for this.

Also look at the story of Joseph again, reflecting further on the key points and allowing for group participants to share what they have written in the response box.

Allow for a good amount of time during the meeting for the Character Friend Triplets (CFT) to meet. This is the second planned meeting during the intensive practice session and instructions are given in the Act section on what they should do.

If you want to have a few moments of fun, give everyone time to search for "self-control memes" on the internet and then share the results. You may even want to make this a small contest of who finds the best meme.

Homework. Participants will need to complete Week 16 before the next meeting.

Check the Further Exploration section for additional resources for this week.

(Further Exploration)[85]

Your notes for this meeting:

Week 16 – Facilitator Guide

(to be used in conjunction with Week 16 in this workbook)

As usual, ask participants for a brief report on their habituation.

Begin with a summary from this lesson on what courage is. Engage in further explanation and discussion around some of the concepts which might be new to participants. For example:

a.   is fear always wrong?

b.   how do we recognize righteous anger, and what instead can make anger wrong?

c.   what makes us discouraged and how do we deal with discouragement?

Look at the story of Joshua again, reflecting further on the key points and allowing for participants to share what they have written in their "Now respond" box.

The Act section of this lesson asked participants to perform an act of courage. Have each share what their fear was – what it was stopping them from doing what was right – and what they did to overcome that fear. Also focus on how they felt during the process.

Broaden this discussion to talk about how it feels to take ownership of our character and intentionally do things, such as a habituation plan, that move us in the direction of specific virtues.

Homework. Participants will need to complete Week 17 before the next meeting.

Check the Further Exploration section for additional resources for this week.

(Further Exploration)[86]

Your notes for this meeting:

Week 17 – Facilitator Guide

(to be used in conjunction with Week 17 in this workbook)

Start with the text on John the Baptist that deals with repentance and justice. Discuss what participants have written about the possible implications for evangelism. Allow for agreement/disagreement.

Discuss further some of the details of the painting *Allegory of Good Government* (you may want to find a way to visually look at this painting during the meeting). Here are some possible questions:

a. What is Concord and how is it connected to Justice?

b. Why is Justice looking up to Wisdom? What might be in the book that Wisdom is holding?

c. Think of the current politicians/rulers in your country. Which of the six virtues sitting next to the Commune can you see? Which are not seen and how is the community damaged because of it?

d. Think of your local church community. How might this painting be applied to good church leadership? What is needed? How might the painting help explain why churches are sometimes poor examples of good community.

Allow at least half of your time for the Character Friend Triplets (CFT) to meet. This is the third planned meeting during the intensive practice session and instructions are given in the Act section.

You may want to raise the apparent tension between justice and forgiveness again in the larger group (it is a point of discussion in the CFTs).

Homework. Participants will need to complete Week 18 before the next meeting.

Check the Further Exploration section for additional resources for this week.

(Further Exploration)[87]

Your notes for this meeting:

Week 18 – Facilitator Guide

(to be used in conjunction with Week 18 in this workbook)

As usual, allow a brief time to report on habituation plans. Perhaps also ask participants whether they feel that the specific lessons on individual virtues (virtue literacy) are having a positive influence on their character.

Go over the Bible study in Matthew 25 again. In particular you may want to focus on the aspect of "works" and discuss the relation of character education with salvation by works and whether an overemphasis on grace and faith might damage our commitment to discipleship.

Discuss the following question: Is there value in giving a drink to the thirsty even if we do not share the gospel with them? The underlying issue in the question is whether works of mercy have worth on their own or are mainly tools of evangelism.

Involve participants in finding biblical texts or stories that speak about compassion and mercy. You may, for example, try to associate the fourteen works of mercy with a story or a verse. You may also want to look up these additional verses on works of mercy: Isaiah 58:6–10; Ezekiel 18:5–9; Proverbs 22:9; Hebrews 13:1–3.

Ask participants to share their responses to the following sections in the lesson:

a. Which works of mercy they are engaged in?

b. Which work of mercy did they perform towards their parents?

c. Which work of mercy do they feel they would like to commit to in the coming months?

Homework. Participants will need to complete Week 19 before the next meeting.

Check the Further Exploration section for additional resources for this week.

(Further Exploration)[88]

Your notes for this meeting:

Week 19 – Facilitator Guide

(to be used in conjunction with Week 19 in this workbook)

Allow a brief time to monitor habituation plans. Ask participants if habituation is starting to become more of a natural habit.

Depending on the participants in your group, there may be some new ideas that have come out of this lesson. Consider taking more time to offer more teaching and space for discussion around the following statements:

a. There are many different activities beyond paid employment that can be considered "work."

b. Work is not an evil but a privileged expression of our human nature.

c. We need to be careful in creating hierarchies between things that are spiritual and material.

d. Discipleship includes our life of work.

Go through the matching exercise in the Bible study section of the lesson, reading each verse and discussing the corresponding statements.

Ask participants to share how they felt about their responses in the Bible study section. What did it feel like to verbalize that their work has value for God?

Talk more about the *Choice of Hercules.* Is this still a relevant parable? Ask participants what they would have chosen and why? Then ask them what most people in your culture would choose and why.

Talk about *orderliness* as a virtue. Ask them if they agree/disagree with the following statement: A person whose room/home/car is dirty and messy is not a good example of Christian discipleship.

Homework. Participants will need to complete Week 20 before the next meeting.

Check the Further Exploration section for additional resources for this week.

(Further Exploration)[89]

Your notes for this meeting:

Week 20 – Facilitator Guide

(to be used in conjunction with Week 20 in this workbook)

Participants have been habituating for ten weeks. Include some time for reporting and comment on how it is going as they enter the final stretch.

Discuss with participants the "allocentric quintet" of virtues and how they work together.

Perform a thought experiment with the group, asking them to imagine what a community or a family would look like in which no one ever expressed any gratitude to anyone.

You might ask to share about how they feel when they are not thanked for something they have done for someone else. Do they feel resentment? What virtues are needed to deal with ingratitude? How did Jesus deal with the nine ungrateful lepers?

Ask participants to share with each other who they said thank you to in the response section of the Bible study. You may want to repeat this during your meeting, encouraging participants to say "thank you" to someone in a special way (e.g. by sending a text message to someone).

This week the Character Friend Triplets are meeting. This is the fourth planned meeting during the intensive practice session and instructions are given in the Act section in Week 20. As usual, leave sufficient time during the meeting for this to happen. Before they meet, ask how these character friendships are working? Are they cultivating generosity, honesty and vulnerability in their interactions?

Homework. Participants will need to complete Week 21 before the next meeting.

Check the Further Exploration section for additional resources for this week.

(Further Exploration)[90]

Your notes for this meeting:

Week 21 – Facilitator Guide

(to be used in conjunction with Week 21 in this workbook)

Begin with a short accountability session on habituation plans.

The capital sin of *acedia* is probably new to most participants in your group. Go through the main points of the lesson and discuss them together. Here are some possible discussion questions:

a. What does it mean that vice is "love gone wrong"? How does the filter of love help us understand virtue and vice? You may want to investigate further on what Augustine wrote in regard to *ordo amoris* and about how vice is understood as disordered love in relation to God, neighbour and the world.

b. Talk about the similarities and differences between acedia and depression, taking care to not go beyond your own understanding of the latter (which can be a very sensitive matter). If there is someone who suffers from depression in your group, this topic might set off reactions that call for professional help.

c. Further elaborate on Plato's three-fold metaphor.

Take some time to investigate and discuss whether acedia is a vice in your context, culture and generation. Discuss whether the list of conditions in which acedia flourishes relate to your cultural context.

Ask participants to share what they have done that was ambitious this week (see Act section).

Read the Bible stories of the Red Sea crossing and of Mary going to the mountain. Focus in particular on the "Now respond" section and ask participants to share about their time spent on social media and on movie series. Is there a problem of wasted time? What is the balance between healthy entertainment and bad habits? Lead in a time of prayer for each other on this specific topic.

Homework. Participants will need to complete Week 22 before the next meeting.

Check the Further Exploration section for additional resources for this week.

(Further Exploration)[91]

Your notes for this meeting:

Week 22 – Facilitator Guide

(to be used in conjunction with Week 22 in this workbook)

This is the final habituation stretch. Ask again for a moment of accountability. Also announce that the coming week is the final week of habituation and encourage participants to complete well.

The topic of the theological virtues is vast. As a group leader you may want to do some research and prepare further teaching on the matter. You may look both at early Christian history and key biblical texts.

Go through the matching exercise of the virtues/vices that describe love in 1 Corinthians. Discuss each one.

You may want to discuss biblical stories that illustrate the theological virtues. For example, where can we see faith in Abraham, hope in Moses and love in David?

Which of the three theological virtues do participants find most challenging?

Go back to the story of the dog Hachikō. Ask in what ways participants have felt like this dog? In what ways would participants wish to be more like Hachikō?

Complete with a collective time of prayer to ask God for the grace of having faith, hope and love in our character.

Homework. Participants will need to complete Week 23 before the next meeting.

Check the Further Exploration section for additional resources for this week.

(Further Exploration)[92]

Your notes for this meeting:

Week 23 – Facilitator Guide

(to be used in conjunction with Week 23 in this workbook)

This week is the final meeting with the Character Friend Triplets (CFT). An outline is provided in the Act section for their time together. Since this is the final meeting of the CFT, allow a little more time than usual as they have additional points to consider.

The virtue of prudence may be one of the more difficult virtues to understand. Take some time to go over the content of the lesson. Elaborate where necessary.

Read Ecclesiastes 3 with the group and ask how this helps us understand the virtue of prudence. Go back over the Bible study on honey and fools and use it to reinforce understanding around the virtue of prudence. Also engage with the story of Martha and discuss the interpretation of this text that is being offered.

Ask each group member to give an example of where they have exercised prudence. Or perhaps, where they have not exercised prudence. This might be drawn from the response box in the lesson.

In Christian discipleship we sometimes find "rule books" that offer us "seven rules for . . ." or "ten steps towards . . ." or "three ways to . . .". These can contain good suggestions, but they can be wrongly taken as inflexible rules. Lead the group in how they might critique these Christian "rule books" in light of the virtue of prudence.

Homework. Ask participants to complete Week 24 before the next final meeting. The reflective writing exercise in Week 24 may take one or two hours to produce, so advise participants that they will need to set aside more time to complete than usual. If participants are unable to complete the writing exercise within a week, consider skipping a meeting for a week to give them more time. It is very important that this writing exercise be completed with sufficient focus.

Check the Further Exploration section for additional resources for this week.

(Further Exploration)[93]

Your notes for this meeting:

Week 24 – Facilitator Guide

(to be used in conjunction with Week 24 in this workbook)

There are several things going on during this final week. Try to give some time to each of them.

Allow time to share the results of the evaluation and second testing. Did participants generally score better than the first time in the Virtue Test? Are they encouraged or discouraged by their results. Were there any surprises? How did they feel as they compared results?

The reflective writing exercise can be very powerful. There will likely not be time for everyone to read everything they have written but allow some time of sharing both about the experience of writing and about what they have written.

Make this an evening of celebration. Perhaps organize an evening of singing, testimonies, thanksgiving and worship. Also ask them to share how they will celebrate personally.

This is your last group meeting on this specific project. You may want to arrange a time of feedback and to discuss your plans as a group.

Your notes for this meeting:

Your feedback as facilitator

At the end of the 24-week project, please share your feedback as a group facilitator with the author of this workbook through the online feedback form below.

(Your Feedback)[94]

This feedback will be used both to improve the dynamic online content and future reprints of the workbook. Please also share any resources that you might come across in your context and culture that might be published in the Further Exploration section.

Further Exploration

Further resources related to the content of this workbook and ideas for additional exploration are made available through the link below.

(Further Exploration)[95]

This is a curated list of resources, including websites, books, videos, images, blogs and podcasts that is regularly updated with new resources by the author.

Indications are also given for chapters in *Character and Virtue in Theological Education* (Langham Global Library, 2019) that provide further theoretical and scholarly depth in relation to many of the topics and issues raised in this workbook.

(Purchase *Character and Virtue in Theological Education*)[96]

Notes

1. *Character and Virtue in Theological Education* is the primary source of the materials in this workbook, that is designed to be a practical companion volume. In the Further Exploration section, indications are given concerning specific chapters of *Character and Virtue in Theological Education* to deepen your insight and theoretical understanding of the topics raised in the workbook. Some materials from the first book have been reused in this fresh context.

2. The structure of the website is similar to this workbook, but the materials are presented for a more general audience (not specifically for Christian discipleship).

3. Answers: (a) true, (b) time, slow, (c) true, (d) true, (e) true, (f) true.

4. James Arthur, Kristján Kristjánsson, Tom Harrison, Wouter Sanderse, Daniel Wright, *Teaching Character and Virtue in Schools* (London: Routledge, 2017), 28.

5. Answers: (a) form, (b) goodness, (c) true, (d) vices, (e) attention, (f) will to action, (g) emotions, (h) desires, (i) expression.

6. Arthur et al., *Teaching*, 28.

7. For example, 2 Peter 1:15 (virtue), Philippians 4:8 (excellent).

8. https://virtueducation.net/wp-content/uploads/2020/12/Virtue-Wheel-Oxenham-1.png

9. Answers: (a) free response, (b) wisdom, holiness, righteousness, sanctification, sin, (c) false, (d) cardinal virtues, (e) intellectual virtues, (f) friendliness, honesty, civility, etc., (g) free response, (h) humility, kindness, patience, diligence, generosity, abstinence/balance, chastity/self-control, (i) sailing, (j) false, (k) false.

10. Answers: (a) telling stories of virtue, (b) envy, (c) righteous, (d) Proverbs, (e) meekness, love of neighbour, hope, courage, faith (other examples are also possible), (f) true, (g) 1 Timothy and Titus, (h) true, (i) Origen, Ambrose, Gregory of Nazianzus, Chrysostom, Augustine, St. Benedict, St. Francis, Abelard, Aquinas, (j) false.

11. Confucius, *The Analects*, 12.22, 15.24, 17.6, Indian University Bloomington website, http://www.indiana.edu/~p374/ Analects_of_Confucius_(Eno-2015).pdf, accessed 15 July 2018.

12. Aristotle, *The Nicomachean Ethics*, trans. William Ross (Los Angeles: Enhanced Media Publishers, 2017), 1.7.

13. Kristján Kristjánsson, *Aristotelian Character Education* (London: Routledge, 2015), 49.

14. Answers: (a) true, (b) any of the following: praise literature, lament literature, codes, myths, epics, wisdom literature, (c) *ren*, (d) *junzi*, (e) Aristotle, (f) true, (g) false, (h) true, (i) false.

15. R. Meye, "Theological Education as Character Formation," *Theological Education*, Supplement 1 (1988).

16. Answers: (a) desires, (b) motivations, (c) vulnerable and accountable, (d) pain, (e) constancy.

17. Answers: (a) humility and prudence, (b) true, (c) true, (d) more extreme, (e) true.

18. https://virtueducation.net/w6/

19. https://virtueducation.net/virtues-unpacked/

20. Answers: (1) i, (2) e, (3) m, (4) b, (5) a, (6) l, (7) c, (8) k, (9) d, (10) f, (11) g, (12) h, (13) j.

21. Answers: (a) false, (b) habituation, (c) character friendship, (d) virtue literacy, (e) intention, (f) false.

22. Answers: (a) true, (b) habits, (c) habits, (d) habits, (e) true, (f) will.

23. Answers: (a) habits, (b) character, (c) it should be Specific, Measurable, Achievable, Relevant and Time-bound, (d) true, (e) twelve.

24. Aristotle, *Nicomachean Ethics*, trans. H. Rackham, Loeb Classical Library 73 (Cambridge: Harvard University Press, 1926), 450–51.

25. Cicero, *How to be a Friend*, trans. P. Freeman (Princeton: Princeton University Press, 2018), 155.

26. Kristján Kristjánsson, "Aristotelian Character Friendship as a 'Method' of Moral Education," *Studies in Philosophy and Education* 38, no. 4 (2020): 349–64.

27. Aristotle, *Nicomachean Ethics*, trans. H. Rackham, Loeb Classical Library 73 (Cambridge: Harvard University Press, 1926), 450–51.

28. Answers: (a) true, (b) good things, (c) utility friendships, pleasure friendships and virtue friendships, (d) true, (e) manipulation, (f) critical.

29. Answers: (a) true, (b) false, (c) peers, (d) criticism, (e) true, (f) true, (g) true.

30. https://virtueducation.net/w6/

31. Answers: (a) true, (b) knowledge, (c) emulation, (d) true, (e) desire, (f) true.

32. John Cassian, *The Sacred Writings of John Cassian: Annotated Edition*, trans. Edgar C. S. Gibson (Altenmünster: Jazzybee Verlag, 2012).

33. Stanley Hauerwas, *The Character of Virtue* (London: Canterbury Press, 2018).

34. Kristján Kristjánsson, Liz Gulliford, James Arthur, Francisco Moller, *Gratitude and Related Character Virtues*, The Jubilee Centre for Character and Virtues (Birmingham: University of Birmingham, 2017), 10.

35. Kharunya Paramaguru, "5 Great Stories About Nelson Mandela's Humility, Kindness and Courage," *Time*, 6 December 2013, https://world.time.com/2013/12/06/5-great-stories-about-nelson-mandelas-humility-kindness-and-courage/.

36. Answers: (a) true, (b) assessment, (c) gratitude, (d) true, (e) pride, (f) self-abasement, (g) true.

37. Answers: (a) true, (b) moderation, self-control, (c) reason, (d) no or enough, (e) meekness, (f) licentiousness, self-indulgence, gluttony, lust, self-denial, asceticism, obsession.

38. Mark Eddy Smith, *Tolkien's Ordinary Virtues* (Downers Grove: InterVarsity Press, 2002).

39. Answers: (a) fears, (b) true, (c) dis-couraged, (d) false, (e) cowardice, (f) imprudence, rashness, foolhardiness or recklessness, (g) hobbits.

40. https://upload.wikimedia.org/wikipedia/commons/c/cd/Ambrogio_Lorenzetti_-_Allegory_of_Good_Government_-_Google_Art_Project.jpg

41. Stanley Hauerwas, *The Character of Virtue* (London: Canterbury Press, 2018).

42. https://afterall.net/quotes/fyodor-dostoevsky-as-ivan-on-justice-and-forgiveness/ (from: *The Brothers Karamazov*, Constance Black Garnett, Trans. (Modern Library: 1977, Orig. November 1880), 254.

43. Answers: (a) true, (b) communal and character, (c) Concord and Wisdom, (d) desire ... due ... interaction ... community, (e) equity, fairness, honesty, obedience to laws, (f) illegality, unfairness, dishonesty, partiality, corruption, tyranny, submissiveness, (g) forgiveness.

44. https://www.goodreads.com/work/quotes/1651617-the-art-of-happiness-a-handbook-for-living, from: Dalai Lama XIV, *The Art of Happiness, A Handbook for Living*. (London: Hodder & Stoughton, 1999).

45. Brian Kolodiejchuk, "For Fr Brian, Mother Teresa's Mercy Is Love in Action that Provokes Us All," *PimeAsiaNews*, 9 July 2016, https://www.asianews.it/notizie-it/P.-Brian:-La-misericordia-di-Madre-Teresa,-amore-in-azione-che-ci-provoca-tutti-38518.html.

46. "Mother Teresa's Moving Tales to Stop Overestimating Our Problems," *Aleteia*, 3 August 2016, https://it.aleteia.org/2016/09/03/racconti-commoventi-libri-madre-teresa-calcutta-rizzoli/.

47. Answers: (a) true, (b) true, (c) true, (d) feeding the hungry, giving drink to the thirsty, sheltering the homeless, visiting the sick, visiting the prisoners, burying the dead, giving alms to the poor, (e) admonishing the sinner, instructing the ignorant, counseling the doubtful, bearing wrongs patiently, forgiving offenses willingly, comforting the afflicted, praying for those in need, (f) disregard, selfishness, indifference, self-annulment.

48. https://en.m.wikipedia.org/wiki/The_Choice_of_Hercules_(Carracci)#/media/File:CarracciHercules.jpg.

49. Divit Metha, "The Choice of Hercules," Medium, 6 July 2022, https://medium.com/@divitmehta/the-choice-of-hercules-f15a8262524e.

50. Answers: (a) false, (b) spiritual and material, (c) true, d) duty, punctuality, orderliness, decency, (e) laziness, sloth, acedia, compulsion, controlling, workaholic attitude.

51. (a) Genesis 3:11, (b) Ecclesiastes 3:10, (c) Genesis 3:17 and Ecclesiastes 1:13, (d) Colossians 3:22, (e) Proverbs 4:10, (f) Colossians 4:1 and Leviticus 19:13, (g) 2 Thessalonians 3:6–12.

52. Cicerco, "M. TVLLI CICERONIS PRO CN. PLANCIO ORATIO," The Latin Library, https://www.thelatinlibrary.com/cicero/plancio.shtml#80. Author's translation.

53. Kristján Kristjánsson, Liz Gulliford, James Arthur, Francisco Moller, *Gratitude and Related Character Virtues*, The Jubilee Centre for Character and Virtues (Birmingham: University of Birmingham, 2017).

54. Seneca, *Moral Letters to Lucilius*, Letter 81 "On Benefits," par 19–21 https://en.wikisource.org/wiki/Moral_letters_to_Lucilius/Letter_81.

55. James Arthur, Kristján Kristjánsson, Liz Gulliford, Blaire Morgan, *An Attitude for Gratitude*, The Jubilee Centre for Character and Virtues (Birmingham: University of Birmingham, 2015), https://www.jubileecentre.ac.uk/wp-content/uploads/2023/05/Attitude_for_Gratitude.pdf.

56. Marcus Aurelius, *Meditations*, First Book, Par XIII https://www.gutenberg.org/cache/epub/2680/pg2680-images.html#link2H_4_0001.

57. Answers: (a) true, (b) forgiveness, humility, generosity, gratitude and compassion, (c) you and others, (d) the Eucharist, (e) true, (f) un-thankfulness, a demanding spirit or complaining.

58. Descriptions drawn and adapted from M. Oxenham, *Liquid Education in Higher Modernity*, (London: Routledge, 2013), 161–62.

59. Answers: (a) pride, envy and wrath, (b) greed, gluttony and lust, (c) acedia, (d) true, (e) false, (f) ambition, (g) the Lion.

60. Wikipedia, s.v. "Hachikō," last modified 5 July 2024, 9:07, https://en.wikipedia.org/wiki/Hachikō.

61. Answers: (a) false, (b) true, (c) Augustine, (d) Aquinas, (e) reliance, reliability and loyalty, (f) joy, friendship, patience.

62. https://en.m.wikipedia.org/wiki/Christ_in_the_House_of_Martha_and_Mary_(Vermeer)#/media/File:Johannes_(Jan)_Vermeer_-_Christ_in_the_House_of_Martha_and_Mary_-_Google_Art_Project.jpg

63. Answers: (a) true, (b) false, (c) true, (d) meta-virtue, (e) stupidity.

64. https://virtueducation.net/w6/

65. Answers: (a) false, (b) true, (c) true.

66. https://virtueducation.net/explore/

67. https://virtueducation.net/your-feedback/

68. https://virtueducation.net/further-exploration/

69. https://virtueducation.net/further-exploration/

70. https://virtueducation.net/add-to-your-faith-virtue-video/

71. https://virtueducation.net/further-exploration/

72. https://virtueducation.net/the-roman-road-to-virtue/

73. https://virtueducation.net/further-exploration/

74. https://virtueducation.net/further-exploration/

75. https://virtueducation.net/further-exploration/

76. https://virtueducation.net/further-exploration/

77. https://virtueducation.net/further-exploration/

78. https://virtueducation.net/further-exploration/

79. https://virtueducation.net/further-exploration/

80. https://virtueducation.net/further-exploration/

81. https://virtueducation.net/further-exploration/
82. https://virtueducation.net/further-exploration/
83. https://virtueducation.net/further-exploration/
84. https://virtueducation.net/further-exploration/
85. https://virtueducation.net/further-exploration/
86. https://virtueducation.net/further-exploration/
87. https://virtueducation.net/further-exploration/
88. https://virtueducation.net/further-exploration/
89. https://virtueducation.net/further-exploration/
90. https://virtueducation.net/further-exploration/
91. https://virtueducation.net/further-exploration/
92. https://virtueducation.net/further-exploration/
93. https://virtueducation.net/further-exploration/
94. https://virtueducation.net/your-feedback/
95. https://virtueducation.net/further-exploration/
96. https://langhamliterature.org/character-and-virtue-in-theological-education

ICETE is a global community, sponsored by nine regional networks of theological schools, to enable international interaction and collaboration among all those engaged in strengthening and developing evangelical theological education and Christian leadership development worldwide.

The purpose of ICETE is:

1. To promote the enhancement of evangelical theological education worldwide.
2. To serve as a forum for interaction, partnership and collaboration among those involved in evangelical theological education and leadership development, for mutual assistance, stimulation and enrichment.
3. To provide networking and support services for regional associations of evangelical theological schools worldwide.
4. To facilitate among these bodies the advancement of their services to evangelical theological education within their regions.

Sponsoring associations include:

Africa: Association for Christian Theological Education in Africa (ACTEA)

Asia: Asia Theological Association (ATA)

Caribbean: Caribbean Evangelical Theological Association (CETA)

Europe: European Council for Theological Education (ECTE))

Latin America: Association for Evangelical Theological Education in Latin America (AETAL)

Middle East and North Africa: Middle East Association for Theological Education (MEATE)

North America: Association for Biblical Higher Education (ABHE)

www.icete-edu.org

Langham Literature and its imprints are a ministry of Langham Partnership.

Langham Partnership is a global fellowship working in pursuit of the vision God entrusted to its founder John Stott –

> *to facilitate the growth of the church in maturity and Christ-likeness through raising the standards of biblical preaching and teaching.*

Our vision is to see churches in the Majority World equipped for mission and growing to maturity in Christ through the ministry of pastors and leaders who believe, teach and live by the word of God.

Our mission is to strengthen the ministry of the word of God through:
* nurturing national movements for biblical preaching
* fostering the creation and distribution of evangelical literature
* enhancing evangelical theological education

especially in countries where churches are under-resourced.

Our ministry

Langham Preaching partners with national leaders to nurture indigenous biblical preaching movements for pastors and lay preachers all around the world. With the support of a team of trainers from many countries, a multi-level programme of seminars provides practical training, and is followed by a programme for training local facilitators. Local preachers' groups and national and regional networks ensure continuity and ongoing development, seeking to build vigorous movements committed to Bible exposition.

Langham Literature provides Majority World preachers, scholars and seminary libraries with evangelical books and electronic resources through publishing and distribution, grants and discounts. The programme also fosters the creation of indigenous evangelical books in many languages, through writer's grants, strengthening local evangelical publishing houses, and investment in major regional literature projects, such as one volume Bible commentaries like *The Africa Bible Commentary* and *The South Asia Bible Commentary*.

Langham Scholars provides financial support for evangelical doctoral students from the Majority World so that, when they return home, they may train pastors and other Christian leaders with sound, biblical and theological teaching. This programme equips those who equip others. Langham Scholars also works in partnership with Majority World seminaries in strengthening evangelical theological education. A growing number of Langham Scholars study in high quality doctoral programmes in the Majority World itself. As well as teaching the next generation of pastors, graduated Langham Scholars exercise significant influence through their writing and leadership.

To learn more about Langham Partnership and the work we do visit **langham.org**

www.ingramcontent.com/pod-product-compliance
Ingram Content Group UK Ltd.
Pitfield, Milton Keynes, MK11 3LW, UK
UKHW021514120225
4561UKWH00036B/1405